P9-CCH-979

MARYLAND

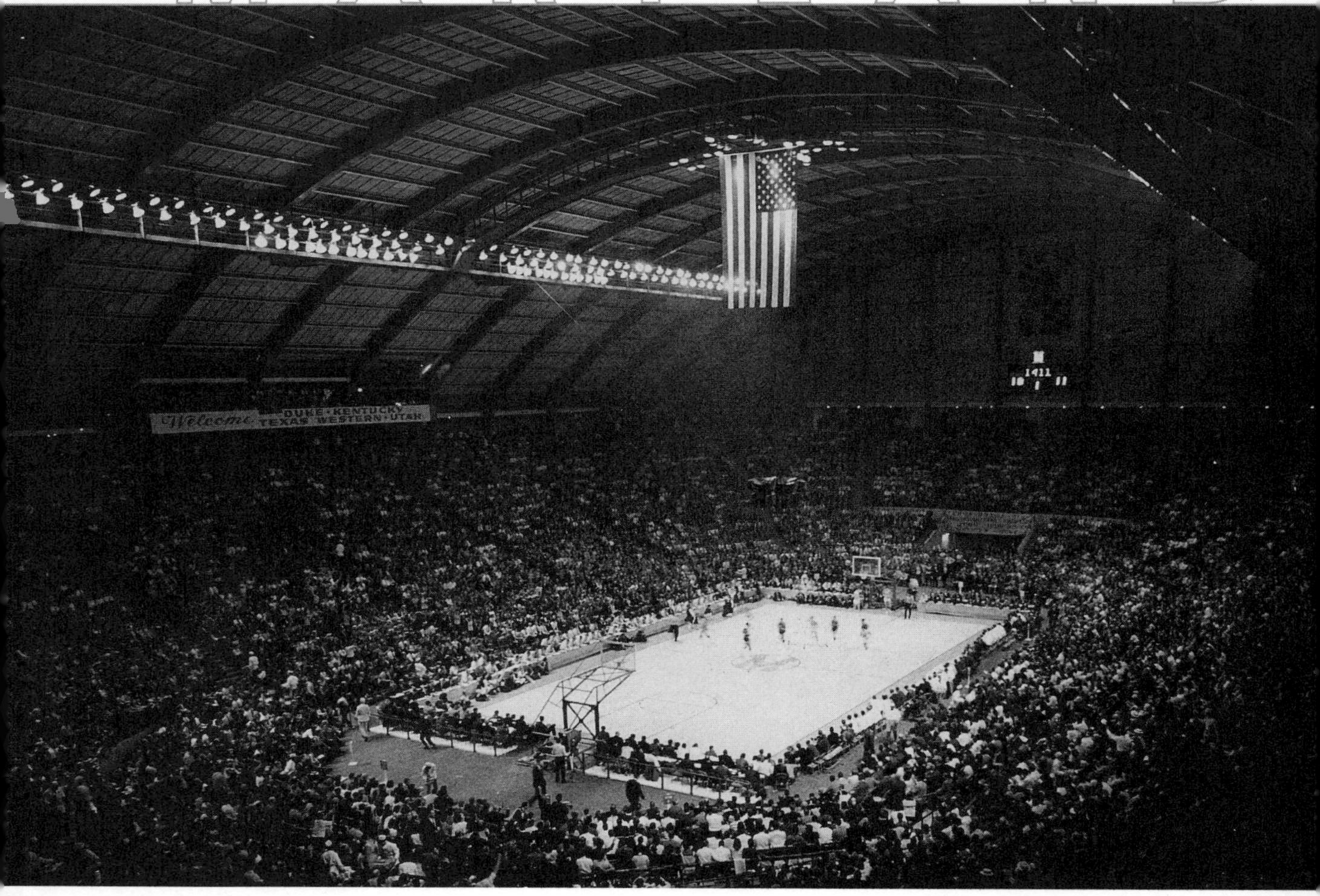

BASKETBALL
TALES FROM COLE FIELD HOUSE

Paul McMullen
with a foreword by Len Elmore

The Johns Hopkins University Press   Baltimore & London

© 2002 The Johns Hopkins University Press
All rights reserved. Published 2002

Printed in the United States of America on acid-free paper
9 8 7 6 5 4 3 2 1

The Johns Hopkins University Press
2715 North Charles Street
Baltimore, Maryland 21218-4363
www.press.jhu.edu

Frontispiece: Cole Field House was spruced up for the 1966 NCAA
Final Four. Texas Western beat Kentucky in a championship game
regarded as one of the most important events in college basketball history.
Courtesy University of Maryland Archives, Hornbake Library.

Library of Congress Cataloging-in-Publication Data
McMullen, Paul, 1955–
    Maryland basketball : tales from Cole Field House / Paul McMullen.
        p.   cm.
    Includes index.
    ISBN 0-8018-7221-9 (hardcover : alk. paper)
    1. University of Maryland (College Park, Md.)—Basketball—History.
2. Maryland Terrapins (Basketball team)—History. I. Title.
GV885.43.U535 M36   2002
796.323′63′0975251—dc21

                                                          2002007589

A catalog record for this book is available from the British Library.

To Mary, for her love and courage

CONTENTS

TRADITION IS, in one sense, the handing down of custom, of lore, from one generation to the next. I have a thirty-two-year association with the University of Maryland. I am a proud alumnus who can claim to have participated as a member of several university boards and committees, but most notably as a student athlete in the early 1970s. This special relationship with my school has allowed me to absorb, reflect, and even make some of the custom and lore that make up Maryland basketball tradition.

This tradition began with the lily-white, crew-cut upstarts who became the 1958 Atlantic Coast Conference Tournament champs. It continued through the Lefty Driesell era of promise and disappointment and the Len Bias tragedy, the ensuing chaos, and the order of the Gary Williams era. Paul McMullen's artful, nostalgic, and sometimes controversial account of Maryland basketball history brings life and clarity to celebrated events and seminal moments of the program, many of which I experienced at first hand. His words are the cord that binds together a story previously known to insiders but largely unknown to those outside the Maryland "family."

Before the amazing 2002 season, I had always maintained that Maryland's basketball tradition was as rich and meaningful as that of any other college program, despite having no NCAA National Championship about which I could boast. After all, it was Maryland that had integrated Atlantic Coast Conference basketball. The university's famed Cole Field House played host to a couple of classic Final Fours, including the historic 1966 Texas Western–Kentucky final game. Our epic battles with North Carolina State in 1974 led to the expansion of the NCAA tournament field the following year.

I always believed that it would take a National Championship for the Maryland basketball chronicle to be fully understood, and credit given to all who have played a role in elevating the Terps to their current lofty status. It was my teams of the early 1970s—Lefty's boys—who started the march toward a championship in earnest. We were ordained, but we never ascended.

Nevertheless, as this book demonstrates, the irony is fitting. Gary Williams, who as a player represented the hard-nosed but unsuccessful programs that had preceded Lefty Driesell, coached the lone National Championship team in 2002, the same year that venerable Cole was closed for good. For me, this convergence of events has brought a mystique and a bit of closure to a story that has run the emotional gamut from dullness to high excitement and from lofty expectations to disappointment, tragedy, and irrelevance. The Terps' achievement of the ultimate college basketball triumph is finally a renaissance, an affirmation of sorts.

If this is your first exposure to the history of basketball in College Park, this book is truly not to be missed. For those of us—athletes and fans alike—who have chosen to be a part of the ever-evolving tradition known as Maryland basketball, it's history worth retelling.

LEN ELMORE

THE UNIVERSITY OF MARYLAND men's basketball program called Cole Field House home for 47 seasons. The first 46 typically ended with nagging questions that usually began with "What if . . . ?" What if Al Bunge had been healthy in 1958, when the Terrapins had made their first appearance in the National Collegiate Athletic Association (NCAA) tournament? What if that tournament had been open to more than one team per conference in 1974, when Maryland had a marvelous collection of talent but wasn't quite good enough to get out of the Atlantic Coast Conference? What if Moses Malone had spent a few seasons in College Park, instead of jumping directly from high school to the pros? What if the Terps had gone a player or two deeper in 1975—or 1980—and not run out of gas? What if Len Bias had not died in 1986, and plunged Maryland into a dark period from which it took years to emerge? What if Lonny Baxter and Terence Morris hadn't gotten into foul trouble at the 2001 Final Four?

For decades the Terps had been the most accomplished program in college basketball that had never been to the Final Four, and when they finally got there in 2001, what should have been a moment of triumph turned into another frustrating experience. When the Terps wasted a 22-point cushion on rival Duke in the NCAA semifinals, Maryland's mark on the Final Four was having blown the biggest lead ever at the sport's showcase event. It was already known as the only member of the Atlantic Coast Conference (ACC) ever to lose three straight ACC tournament finals, and the collapse crystallized Maryland's what-if track record and tested the patience of its fans, who could relate to Charlie Brown. Their Terps were Lucy, and their championship dreams were her football. Every time poor Charlie tried to kick it through the uprights, she yanked the ball away and he wound up flat on his back. There were dozens of instances when Terp fans wanted to stomp their feet like Lefty Driesell, or fling their sport coats like Gary Williams.

So many of the Terrapins' recruits and teams had been unable to fulfill expectations, so it was ironic that when Maryland and its long-suffering fans finally rejoiced in an NCAA title in 2002, it was accomplished with players whose arrival in College Park had been accompanied by skepticism. Juan Dixon had not been supposed to succeed in big-time college basketball. Neither had Lonny Baxter. They provided some fascinating story angles, but compelling characters were nothing new to Maryland basketball.

There had been Bud Millikan, the coach charged with invigorating the program, and Billy Jones, one of his recruits, who had become the first African American player in the Atlantic Coast Conference. There had been Driesell, who had arrived in 1969 and screamed, "LOOK AT US!" There had been two of Driesell's most famous players, Tom McMillen, who would become a Rhodes scholar and U.S. congressman, and Bias, whose death would shake Maryland for years. Williams, who had played for Millikan, began to rebuild the program, a process that reached unprecedented heights thanks to Dixon, whose family had experienced the ravages of substance abuse that had afflicted Bias and other Terps.

Maryland basketball has been a rare unifying force in a state that has historically been in conflict with itself. Situated south of the Mason-Dixon Line, Maryland had sided with the North during the Civil War. People in Georgia and North Carolina consider it a northern state. New York and New Jersey view it as a southern state. One of the smallest states in area, Maryland is fractured by distinct boundaries, some geographic, others political. The Land of Pleasant Living is made inviting by the Chesapeake Bay, but parts of western Maryland lie on the other side of the eastern Continental Divide. When he was governor, William Donald Schaefer angered his constituents on the Eastern Shore with a slur that family newspapers reworked into "the outhouse side of the [Bay] Bridge." Power brokers from the suburban Washington, D.C., counties, Montgomery to the north and Prince George's to the east, eye the motives of their counterparts from Baltimore with suspicion, and vice versa.

The populace's sporting allegiances are just as diverse. In College Park, it seems that half of the students root for the New York Yankees instead of the Baltimore Orioles. From the state's mountains to its shore, you can sit on a barstool and find the guy on your left wearing a Baltimore Ravens cap and the guy on your right decked out in Washington Redskins paraphernalia. Unless he's in a Pittsburgh Steelers T-shirt. Ravens coach Brian Billick discovered that on February 20, 2001, before Maryland played North Carolina State at Cole. A few weeks earlier his team had won Super Bowl XXXV, and when Billick was called on take a bow, he was met with as many boos as cheers. Backing the Terps was probably the only thing that crowd could agree on.

That evening Maryland was home for the first time since losing to Florida State. It beat N.C. State, and began a push that would close Cole with 18 straight wins and take the Terps to two straight Final Fours. On the second trip the Terps would bring home an NCAA title, and deliver a most improbable conclusion to the story of Maryland basketball in the Cole era.

THE INSPIRATION FOR THIS BOOK came on February 19, 2000, when Baltimore Washington International Airport was fogged in and University of Maryland booster Jack Heise and I found ourselves rushing to find alternate transportation to Winston-Salem, North Carolina. The Terrapins basketball team had a 4 P.M. game scheduled that afternoon against Wake Forest. I rented the largest car possible, and over the next six hours and 370 miles, Jack sat in the passenger seat and told stories about Maryland basketball. The 1986 death of Len Bias had cast a long shadow over Maryland athletics. For years it seemed inappropriate for former Terp coaches and players to tell "war stories." But with plans under way to construct the Comcast Center, which would be the program's new home, it seemed like a good time to let those men themselves tell the story of Maryland basketball during the Cole Field House era, from 1955 to 2002.

The following winter, I set out to gather the recollections of former Maryland players, coaches, and people who supported the program or followed it closely. On successive days in March 2001, while in Atlanta for the second weekend of the NCAA tournament, I visited the homes of Bud Millikan, the Terps' coach from 1950 to 1967, and Lefty Driesell, their coach from 1969 to 1986. I found both men helping their wives, Millikan raking leaves and Driesell cleaning out his garage. During my years on the Maryland basketball beat for the *Baltimore Sun,* coach Gary Williams often had finished interviews with a reference to the 1960s or 1970s. I am indebted to those three head coaches, and to all of the current and former Terrapin assistant coaches who shared their thoughts.

The research for this book included interviews with approximately four dozen Maryland players, from Gene Shue, their first All-American after World War II, to Juan Dixon and his teammates on the 2001–2002 team. Every player who agreed to an interview was helpful, and several were particularly generous with their time and sentiments. John Sandbower, Jay McMillen, Joe Harrington, Len Elmore, Tom Roy, Greg Manning, Keith Gatlin, and Dave Dickerson were extremely forthcoming, and Mo Howard was my MVP. I'm glad that I followed Billy Hahn's advice and talked to Mo.

Unless otherwise noted, all quotations are from my interviews.

Before interviewing any players and coaches, I visited Jack Zane, the executive director of the university's athletic Walk of Fame, whose service to Maryland predates Cole Field House. Jack opened his library and memory to me, and my only regret is that his longtime co-worker in the Maryland sports information department, Joe F. Blair, was not alive to share his observations. Zane loaned me his copy of George H. Callcott's *A History of the University of Maryland,* the definitive work on the development and growth of the institution. My understanding of Harold C. "Curley" Byrd's ill-fated gubernatorial bid came from Callcott's book. C. Fraser Smith's book *Lenny, Lefty, and the Chancellor,* an excellent account of the scandal that followed the death of Bias, was also particularly illuminating. My knowledge of developer James W. Rouse and his planned city of Columbia was provided by former Towson University professor Guy Sedlack, in his Urban Sociology course.

Background material was found in the *Baltimore Sun,* the *Washington Post,* and the *Washington Times,* and in several defunct newspapers, the *Evening Sun* and the *News American* in Baltimore and the *Washington Star.* Dates, facts, and spellings were checked in media guides produced by the National Collegiate Athletic Association, the Atlantic Coast Conference, the University of Maryland, and Maryland's opponents. Several themes were initially explored in articles that I wrote for the *Sun,* where the legwork offered by researchers Jean Packard and Paul McCardell is renowned. Former Maryland athletic director Jim Kehoe loaned a scrapbook; Molly Dunham, the former executive sports editor of the *Sun,* shared her extensive files from the late 1970s and early 1980s; and Paul Baker offered additional archival material and his keen observations of high school and college basketball in the mid-Atlantic region. Buzz Sawyer loaned his 1946 Granby High School yearbook, and Drew Schaufler allowed me to borrow a publicity still from 1955, when Cole opened.

Assistance was also provided by Douglas P. McElrath and Anne S. K. Turkos of the university's Hornbake Library; Dave Haglund, Kevin Messenger, and Jason Yellin of the university's media relations staff; former Maryland sports information director Chuck Walsh; Mary Lucas, who provided the boys' basketball database of the Maryland Public Secondary Schools Athletic Association; and Cleo Thomas-Long, the administrative assistant to Williams, who offered a phone directory of former Terps. All saved me many hours.

This book would not have been possible without the advice of friends and acquaintances. Ken Denlinger, John Eisenberg, Ted Patterson, and Gregg Wilhelm explained the publishing business to a first-time author. Andy Knobel supplied his sharp proofreading skills, and Brad Snyder's expertise was priceless. Hunter S. Thompson had his 300-pound Samoan attorney; I've got Brad.

I appreciate the patience of Bob Brugger and Melody Herr of the Johns Hopkins University Press, as we worked within an extraordinarily tight time frame on a story that did not have an ending until April 1, 2002. Thanks to Williams, Dixon, Lonny Baxter, and the rest of the Terrapins for providing a most exciting conclusion.

WHEN THE UNIVERSITY OF MARYLAND kissed Cole Field House good-bye in March 2002 and opened the Comcast Center, the move did not come cheap. The university came up with $48.4 million, which included a $25 million payment from a Philadelphia-based communications empire for the naming rights. The State Highway Administration spent nearly $18 million to construct a parking garage and build roads to the complex on the north side of the campus in College Park. The state coffers produced another $60.6 million.

The project enjoyed a fast track, and Maryland Athletic Director Debbie Yow was effusive in her thanks for all of that cash and cooperation. Parris Glendening, a former professor in College Park, was the state's governor during the center's approval and construction. The university was located in Prince George's County, the political base of State Senate President Mike Miller, who championed the Comcast Center. There had been no substantial scrutiny of or protest over an expenditure that would run more than $127 million. Maryland's prominent men's basketball program had outgrown Cole, where tickets were hard to come by. But the building of Comcast was in great contrast to the opening of Cole.

The old field house had grown antiquated and out of compliance with federal regulations regarding accessibility by 2002, but 47 years earlier it had been hailed as a basketball palace. It was the second-largest arena on the East Coast, behind only a contemporary version of Manhattan's Madison Square Garden. It would be 15 years before its home-court advantage would be completely realized, but its sight lines were unobstructed and superb, and high school players from small towns and big cities alike were awestruck when they walked into the mammoth bowl. When it opened in 1955, however, one big question loomed over the construction of Cole Field House: Why?

Scalpers got more than $1,000 for the final games at Cole, but in the early 1950s basketball was not a big deal in College Park and there was little demand to erect what might have been the premier on-campus arena in the United States. The Atlantic Coast Conference didn't exist, Maryland had never been to the NCAA tournament, and there was nothing to suggest the passion that the game would one day generate across the state and the mid-Atlantic region.

In 1947–48, the second National Basketball Association (NBA) title went to the Baltimore Bullets, who were disbanded early in the 1954–55 season. The Washington Capitols went to the NBA finals in 1948–49, but the franchise folded in the middle of the 1950–51 season. Collegiately, the game hadn't offered much of a winter diversion in the region. In 1949 Jim Lacy of little Loyola College became the first player in NCAA history to score 2,000 points. Georgetown (1943) and George Washington (1954) made appearances in the NCAA tournament. In Annapolis, coach Ben Carnevale built a regional power at the U.S. Naval Academy that tattooed the Terrapins of Maryland eight straight times from 1944 to 1951.

Burt Shipley was in charge of University of Maryland basketball from 1923 to 1947. That's the longest tenure of any Terp coach, but Shipley first had been a football hero, and his name was attached not to a basketball court but to the Maryland baseball stadium. He coached the baseball team for 37 seasons, and oversaw basketball for 24 remarkably quiet ones.

Basketball's status in College Park finally began to grow in 1950, when Harold C. "Curley" Byrd and Jim Tatum decided that Maryland needed another strong team to complement the football power they had built. Byrd masterminded the transformation of a humble agricultural school into a university, which he constructed from the athletic department up. Byrd was president of the university from 1935 until he ran for governor of the state in 1954, but before that he had coached Terp football from 1911 to 1934. Six coaches and 13 years later, Tatum arrived and made that program one of the nation's best, mighty enough to win a national championship in 1953.

After three seasons at the helm of Maryland basketball, Flucie Stewart went back to coaching football in 1950, and the Terp hierarchy of Byrd and Athletic Director Tatum began a search for the program's first full-time coach. Following the lead of North Carolina State, Maryland looked west.

N.C. State had tapped the state of Indiana's basketball tradition in 1946, when it had hired Everett Case. Through 18 seasons, 377 wins, and ten regular-season conference championships, Case showed "Tobacco Road," the colleges concentrated in the state, how to play basketball and made the University of North Carolina and Duke University take the sport more seriously. To understand the fervor and fundamentals that Case brought to Raleigh, watch the 1986 film *Hoosiers,* which depicts basketball's revered status in Indiana. Case won nearly 500 games in Indiana's

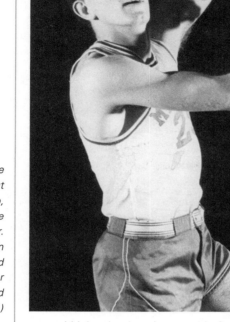

Gene Shue had come to Maryland without an athletic scholarship, but left in 1954 as the program's best player. Shue set a Terrapin career scoring record that would stand for two decades. (Maryland Sports Information.)

rugged high school environment before he went to Raleigh and led N.C. State to build spacious Reynolds Coliseum in 1949.

Other family trees grew in college basketball. At Oklahoma State University, Henry Iba would win 767 games and nurture coaches like Don Haskins and Eddie Sutton, and it was his office in Stillwater that Tatum called when he needed a coach who could put the Terps on the college basketball map. Iba recommended a former student and assistant coach, Herman A. "Bud" Millikan.

Millikan had been raised in Maryville, Missouri, where much of his spare time had been spent at the local state teachers college. The coach there was Iba, a fellow native of the Show Me State. When Iba went to Stillwater, he called back to Maryville and recruited Millikan, who played basketball for the Cowboys as the decade changed from the 1930s to the 1940s. Like all male students at what was then called Oklahoma A&M, Millikan was in the ROTC, the Reserve Officers' Training Corps, but he was not put in harm's way during World War II.

"I was asthmatic," Millikan said. "I had a real bad attack on a train pulling into Muskogee one day, sat in the hospital for a while, and was discharged. That's why I say I fought the battle of the Mississippi."

Discharged in 1944, Millikan returned to Stillwater for his master's degree and to help the basketball team. In his first season as a coach, Oklahoma A&M won the NCAA tournament. In NCAA media guides that chronicle the history of the tournament, the last man on the right in the team photo of the Cowboys' 1945 champions is misidentified as "Bobby Milikan," an erroneous transcription of Iba's pet name for his protégé.

"Mr. Iba always called me Buddy," Millikan said. "Every coach you ever have, you gain something from. I gained the world from him."

While Iba took Oklahoma A&M to another NCAA title in 1946 and to the championship game in 1949, Millikan moved on to teach and coach at high schools in his Missouri hometown and Iowa. He was considering another line of work when his life was changed a second time by a phone call from Iba.

"Mr. Iba called and said I was going to get a phone call from Jim Tatum," Millikan said. "Maxine [Millikan's wife] and I talked, said it was a long way from where we are. We had always lived in the Midwest, but I had always said if I wasn't into college coaching after seven or eight years, I was going to get out of the business. I didn't just want to teach high school. In college, our basketball team made a trip east every December. In my sophomore year (1939–40), we played Duke in Baltimore, but I had never been to College Park. Before I went for the interview, I had to get an atlas and study the map, because all I knew was that it was in the state of Maryland. During my visit, Jim Tatum took me into Curley Byrd's office. He said, 'Young man, can you win some basketball games here?' I said, 'Dr. Byrd, I wouldn't be here if I didn't think I could.' He said, 'Tatum, we ought to hire that guy.'"

While waiting for a firm offer from Maryland, Millikan was offered the coaching position at Southwest Missouri State. After their return from College Park, Millikan and his wife were driving home from the airport when a radio bulletin reported that he had accepted the job at what was then Springfield State.

"I had not, but Jim Tatum was on the phone to me the next morning," Millikan said. "He was a funny man, the way he talked, with a little cough. He said, 'When you were out here, I was talking to a high school coach. Now that I'm talking to a college coach, I can offer you more money.' Mr. Iba recommended that it would be easier to move to a bigger and better job from Maryland than a teachers college in Missouri, so we went to Maryland."

Millikan had gone from assisting the NCAA champions to coaching at a high school in Iowa, but the small-town gyms he worked at looked lavish compared to Maryland's.

"I had to tell Maxine that some of the things about Maryland aren't the greatest," Millikan said. "You don't have the scholarships other schools have. We didn't have any ball racks, just stored them in boxes that the equipment guy reinforced with tape. You had a situation where boxing and basketball are on the same bill as a doubleheader, and that's not attractive. They had a collapsible ring, and they would push it toward the far end of the floor. We didn't have any more doubleheaders after I got there. We had played in some high school gyms that were better than Ritchie Coliseum."

Situated on the east side of U.S. Route 1, just south of the main entrance into campus, Ritchie had been built in 1931, just in time for Maryland's first basketball All-American, Louis "Bosey" Berger. A 1997 renovation made it a fine home for women's volleyball, and on most nights in the early 1950s its seating capacity of 1,500 was plenty for men's basketball.

Byrd had already begun plotting to build a modern arena, but before it became a reality in 1955, two events heightened the awareness of Maryland basketball. Millikan engineered the first, Tatum the second.

Shortly after Millikan arrived on campus in 1950, Gene Shue came down from Baltimore. A lean 6-foot-2 perimeter player, Shue enrolled at Maryland without a scholarship but scored 1,386 points in three varsity seasons. Two decades later, Tom McMillen would finally better that school record and Baltimore would at long last be discovered as a mother lode of talent, but in 1950 it was a basketball backwater. Shue had a strong game and a direct approach, which he wanted to take to Georgetown.

"I was very thin, didn't have a good body but I always had great confidence in my ability," said Shue, who played ten years in the NBA and coached the Baltimore Bullets and Philadelphia 76ers to the league's championship finals. "I tried out at Georgetown twice, but couldn't get a decision out of them. Even a school like Loyola didn't even bother to contact me. I was drawing very little interest, so I went to Maryland for a tryout."

While he waited for a scholarship offer from the Hoyas, Shue was put through his paces by Millikan, a standard practice in an era when recruiting rules were flimsy and coaches were allowed to watch prospects work out against their own players.

"I had Gene shoot around a little bit at Ritchie," Millikan said. "Years afterward, Gene told me, 'I'm surprised you didn't have me do much.' I didn't need to. I knew immediately that we wanted him, but I was worried. He was really interested in Georgetown, and he was a Catholic boy. Years later, I tried to recruit another Catholic boy, out of St. Cecilia's in

New Jersey. His mother told him that Catholic boys go to Catholic schools, and he ended up going to La Salle."

That good Catholic boy was Bill Raftery, the CBS analyst.

Turned down by Georgetown, Shue headed to College Park. While he played on the freshman team in 1950–51, Millikan turned the remnants of a squad that had gone 7-18 under Stewart into one that went 16-11.

"That was one of the greatest coaching jobs I have ever seen," Shue said. "He did not have that much talent, but Bud molded that group into a fantastic team. It overachieved, kept getting better and better. Bud was the guy who really made the basketball program into something."

Byrd and Tatum gave basketball an inadvertent nudge in 1951, when the Terps' unbeaten football team accepted a bid to the January 1952 Sugar Bowl, in defiance of a Southern Conference ban on bowl games. That ban had been precipitated by scandals in basketball, as point shaving had tainted Kentucky's run of three NCAA titles in four years and had led several New York powers to drop the sport. The bowl ban would keep sports in the proper perspective, but the Southern Conference's larger schools were in no mood to comply with what they had considered a sanctimonious gesture. Maryland beat Tennessee in New Orleans to complete its only perfect season in the 20th century, Clemson went to the Gator Bowl, and the football powers rumbled that they had outgrown the Southern Conference.

Basketball had also become unwieldy in the 17-team league, where Shue and Furman's Frank Selvy, one of the stars of the day, never met once. Barred from playing football in the Southern Conference in 1952 because he defied the bowl ban, Tatum played a national schedule. A year later, Maryland and seven other members broke away to form the ACC. Tatum's football team won the national championship in 1953, and Terps basketball began to blossom, too.

In 1952–53, Maryland's last season in the Southern Conference, the Terps went 15-8 and Shue scored 22.1 points a game, a mark that would stand as the Terps' school record for 16 years. He was the most valuable player of the Southern Conference tournament in 1953, as a school-record 40 points he scored in a semifinal loss to Wake Forest won over the media who had not included Shue on their all-conference team. His senior season coincided with the birth of the ACC in 1953–54, when Shue led the conference in field-goal percentage, repeated as a second-team All-American, and got the Terps their first appearance in the national Top 20 after a big win over George Washington. Wake Forest's Dickie Hemric narrowly beat out Shue to become the first ACC Player of the Year and begin Maryland's howling about a Tobacco Road bias against the Terps, who knew who their leader was.

"I underwent an initiation at Maryland," said John Sandbower, who was recruited by Millikan on Shue's recommendation. "Gene and Ralph Greco, who had been an All-American quarterback at Aliquippa High in Pennsylvania, played me and another freshman two-on-two at Ritchie. Ralph loved to play defense and rebound. Gene was hard-nosed, too, and he and Ralph beat us up. I don't know if they did that to the other freshmen, but it was a rite of passage for me."

When Tom Young came to campus for a tryout in 1951, the reception had been similar.

"Bud would have 10 to 15 different high school kids and some Maryland players on the floor," Young said. "We would play for two days running. We would play two-on-two, five-on-five, play every afternoon. One guy who challenged everyone was Gene. He was so tough to play against. He wanted to beat you 10-0 instead of 10-1. He wasn't just a scorer. When he was a sophomore, Gene would guard the other team's best offensive player. Dick Groat at Duke was a great offensive player, and Gene gave him fits. The next year, Bud wouldn't put Gene on the other team's best scorer, because he had become our best scorer. He could shoot, defend, and was a fierce competitor."

Shue exited as the star of the first Maryland team to win 20 games. The foundation that Millikan had built was such that in 1954–55, with Shue gone to the NBA, Maryland broke into the Top 10 and posted a 68-64 victory over No. 2 N.C. State.

"Everett Case deserves a world of credit for the popularity of basketball in North Carolina and the ACC," Millikan said. "You know good and well that Duke, North Carolina, and Wake Forest were not going to sit there forever and take a beating from State."

If Case hadn't come along, would North Carolina have hired New Yorker Frank McGuire as its coach in 1952? Would Maryland have gone ahead and broken ground on its new Student Activities Center? The Wolfpack had a showcase in glamorous Reynolds Coliseum, and Maryland's 68-64 win over State on January 13, 1955, was evidence that there might actually be justification for that massive construction project across Route 1 and up the hill.

"That's the maddest I ever got at Jim Tatum," Millikan said. "That was the second year for the ACC, and in the first season there hadn't been a round robin, so it was N.C. State's first ACC game at Maryland. Man, tickets, you couldn't get any. The place was sold out, and Tatum went on the

radio and said, 'If you don't have a ticket, don't come.' I got so cotton-
pickin' mad. I said, 'Jim, we finally got people real interested in coming
to a basketball game. I don't care if they're lined up Route 1 in both direc-
tions to Baltimore and D.C., I'd love to see them fighting to get in. Let's
don't chase them away.'"

2

AFTER WORLD WAR II, two empire builders from the Eastern Shore of Maryland altered the sociological and educational landscape of the state. One would be hailed as an innovative visionary, the other derided as a dangerous schemer.

James W. Rouse was a native of Easton who studied law and mastered the mortgage business before trying his hand as a real estate developer. In the late 1950s, midway between Baltimore and Annapolis, he built the second enclosed shopping center in the United States, and his project at Harundale would be a landmark in the malling of America. Two decades later, Rouse leveled some run-down wharves on Baltimore's waterfront and built Harborplace.

Rouse didn't begin all of his projects with publicity agents and press releases. In 1963, with a $23 million loan from an insurance company, Rouse set up six dummy corporations and went about secretly purchasing land in the middle of Howard County, a sleepy jurisdiction that served as a buffer between the suburbs of Baltimore and Washington. Eventually, Rouse informed the county that he held the deed to 22 square miles of property, nearly one-tenth of the county. Howard was dotted with family farms that dated to colonial times, and some in the ruling class wanted to keep the county that way. Rouse offered two options: My holdings can be developed willy-nilly, which would lead to uncontrolled sprawl and ugly bedroom communities, or you can follow my blueprint for a utopia that will attract a diverse cross section of races and faiths.

That's how the planned city of Columbia came to be.

The Great Depression forced Rouse to leave the University of Virginia, and he attended the University of Maryland's law school in Baltimore before passing the state bar exam. The other mover and shaker spent nearly his entire adult life in College Park, where a college campus spread its tentacles according to his blueprints.

Harold C. "Curley" Byrd was born in Crisfield in 1889, and over a century later its waterfront heritage is evoked by the mascot of the town's high school: the "Crabber." Motorized transportation was a novelty in

1905, and students from the Eastern Shore ferried across the Chesa-peake en route to Maryland's campus in that year. When Byrd resigned his presidency of the university in 1954 for an ill-fated run at the gover-nor's mansion, College Park was in the midst of a massive expansion that he had orchestrated. Without Byrd's daring, Cole Field House most definitely would not have been built on a scale that was grand for 1955.

With editorial writers at the *Sun* leading the suspicious chorus in Baltimore, Byrd was often criticized for giving lip service to academics. He was revered in athletic circles, however, and his supporters couldn't understand why their claim that he was the only man to rise from the football coach of a college to its presidency was used to belittle his accomplishments.

Nick Davis, John Sandbower, Bob Kessler, Bob O'Brien, and Drew Schaufler (left to right) posed for a publicity still a few weeks before the inaugural game at Cole Field House. John Nacincik replaced Davis in the starting lineup for the opener against Virginia. (Drew Schaufler.)

Byrd was one of the original big men on campus. He pitched for the baseball team, set a school record of 10.0 seconds in the 100-yard dash, and in 1907 captained the football team at what was then the Maryland Agricultural College. Byrd graduated with an engineering degree the following spring, second in his class. The bureaucracy of the NCAA hadn't been formed and eligibility rules hadn't been codified, so Byrd went on to play football for George Washington University and Georgetown, and to run track for Western Maryland College. He took charge of the Maryland football team late in the 1911 season, and ran it through 1934.

He coached through World War I and two name changes for the school, to Maryland State College in 1916 and then to the University of Maryland in 1920. Byrd had 122 wins, 86 losses, and 16 ties over those 24 seasons, and he still holds the Terps' records for longevity and victories, despite the hours he spent on his job as a sports reporter for the defunct *Washington Star*. Byrd lost four of his last five games to Western Maryland College, and while his public college had a promising location, its campus wasn't any more impressive than the one at the equally small private school in Westminster.

Byrd shaped nearly every facet of Maryland's identity. In 1921 he took to calling the student newspaper the *Diamondback*. In 1933 the terrapin, an Eastern Shore delicacy, became the mascot at his suggestion. Two years later, he became president of the university, which was transformed after World War II by a boom of students and then buildings. When Byrd became president in 1935, the College Park campus numbered 2,000 students, an enrollment not much greater than the 1,420 studying at the university's professional schools in Baltimore. When he stepped down in 1954, College Park had nearly 10,000 students.

The school's growing pains were severe, as professors howled about Byrd's placing a priority on athletic luxuries before academic necessities. In George H. Callcott's book *A History of the University of Maryland,* the history professor explored the machinations that led to an expansion that included the building of Cole. It led to an identity crisis that endangered the college.

"We were in the basketball big time with Cole Field House, but Curley did it at the expense of other things," said Callcott 36 years after the 1966 publication of his definitive history. "Curley built Cole Field House instead of a library. The year it was built, the university was threatened with loss of its accreditation. Nobody except Curley knows exactly how the college paid for it."

Jack Heise, for more than six decades a dedicated booster of Maryland athletics, attended high school at Baltimore City College and had his sophomore year at Maryland interrupted by World War II. He piloted B-24 bombing runs out of England, then returned to the campus along with thousands of veterans. The men in what would come to be called "the Greatest Generation" took advantage of the GI Bill, payment for education in recognition of service to their country.

"Curley decided to accept every graduate of a Maryland high school," Heise said. "He charged everyone on the GI Bill in-state tuition, then billed the government the out-of-state fee. He put that additional money in an escrow account for several years. That was the seed money for Cole."

How much did Byrd's end-run accounting get out of the federal government? "The Government Auditing Office," Callcott wrote in 1966, "stumbled on facts indicating that the United States Veterans Administration was being charged not only out-of-state fees for Maryland veterans on the GI Bill, but extra fees beyond that—a total of about $2 million. No one understood the University's bookkeeping, and the government decided the institution was technically within legal bounds, but the episode left an unpleasant memory."

Byrd made extensive land purchases during his presidency, and athletics was prominent in his master plan. The golf course that opened in 1959 was built on land bought with football bowl game guarantees. The familiar bowl at Byrd Stadium, constructed to satisfy Jim Tatum's burgeoning football program, was dedicated in September 1950. Millikan had arrived on campus earlier that year, and while his Maryland basketball team was cramped in Ritchie Coliseum, there wasn't enough interest in the sport to warrant a showcase that would run $3.2 million when the cost of the nearby student union was included.

Basketball games at Ritchie didn't always sell out, but graduation ceremonies were beginning to attract crowds of 15,000. The threat of rain falling on all those students in caps and gowns and their families was cited as part of the rationale to build an arena with 12,230 permanent seats and floor space for more than another 4,000.

"The university needed a convention-type building," Millikan said five decades after his first season with the Terps. "It was in the plans before I ever went to Maryland. When we went from Ritchie to Cole, we lost a hell of a home-court advantage. It was built for big conventions, and graduation exercises. It was not built for basketball."

Before it got a roof, Cole Field House was a selling point to recruits. Drew Schaufler was shown "this big hole in the ground" when he traveled from Philadelphia to visit the campus in 1953. During the next two years, players followed the progress of the construction project. With the arena near completion, some battled vertigo to scurry across the catwalk above the center court line, the platform that would be used for overhead photographs.

The 1955–56 college basketball season concluded in Evanston, Illinois, where Bill Russell and K. C. Jones led the University of San Francisco to a second straight NCAA championship. In College Park it began on December 2, 1955, when the Terps surpassed every other college in the land when it came to gym space.

"We were coming off of another [ACC] championship in football, and Cole kind of put the place on the map," Schaufler said. "The only good gym we were used to playing in was Reynolds Coliseum, at N.C. State. Wake Forest was a dump, there were dirt streets in Winston-Salem, and it looked like the Civil War was still being fought. Clemson was like going to the moon, worse than a high school gym."

Senior Bob Kessler was the top player back from a team that had finished third in the ACC in 1955, but the Terps weren't sure what to expect as they prepared to open the campaign against rival Virginia. For the inaugural game at Cole, Kessler was joined in the starting lineup by sophomore John Nacincik, juniors Bob O'Brien and Schaufler, and a fellow senior, John Sandbower, the captain, who had the privilege of leading Maryland out of its locker room and through the tunnel. An estimated crowd of 9,500 that included Governor Theodore R. McKeldin waited to see if the team was as spectacular as its surroundings.

Sandbower had played on fan metal backboards at Milford Mill High in Baltimore County, where interscholastic athletics were not emphasized. The Terps had practiced in Cole, but now thousands of people, more than any of them had ever played in front of, were watching.

"The place looked like Texas when I walked out of our little locker room and came running out of that tunnel," Sandbower said the year Cole

Bob O'Brien attempting a free throw. The junior from McMechen, West Virginia, scored 15 points in Maryland's 67-55 victory over Virginia on December 2, 1955, opening night at Cole Field House. (Hornbake Library.)

The movement of cheerleaders and fans was restricted in 1955. There were no seats for spectators on the Cole floor until the 1970s. (Hornbake Library.)

closed. "It looked like the whole university was there. I knew that I was very proud of the fact that I led the team out of the tunnel and on to the floor. I remember a whole lot of noise as we were coming out of the chute. The pep band played the fight song, and that always got my juices flowing. My mother and father were there. Afterward they took me out to dinner at the Hot Shoppes on Route 1. I couldn't eat for a long time, I was so high."

Kessler, who finished with 23 points, had the first points at Cole. Field goals by Sandbower and Kessler broke a 30-30 tie just before halftime. With O'Brien adding 15, Maryland didn't look back en route to a 67-55 victory.

Opposing coaches were so eager to see the new arena that opened under the name Student Activities Building that the Terps didn't play on the road until after New Year's Day. Kentucky and its no-nonsense coach, Adolph Rupp, came through on December 15, when the Wildcats became the first visiting team to win at Cole. Two days later, the arena had its first sellout, and the Terps fell again, to North Carolina. The losing streak reached three games on December 29, when Michigan State beat the home team in Maryland's Mid-Winter Festival. The Spartans dropped the championship to George Washington the next day, when the Terps rebounded with a victory over St. Francis of Loretto. That began a five-game winning streak, but Maryland went 7-7 in the ACC and was whipped by Duke in the first round of the ACC tournament to end a 14-10 season.

On December 14, 1956, the arena was rededicated in the name of Judge William P. Cole, Jr., who had earned an engineering degree from the university in 1910, two years after Byrd had done the same. A former U.S. congressman, Cole had chaired the university's Board of Regents since 1944. Nowhere did it bear the name, but in time the arena came to be called Cole Field House.

Byrd thought big, and he dreamed of being the governor at the ribbon-cutting ceremonies at Cole. After four years of posturing and appropriations fights with Governor McKeldin, he resigned his presidency of the university in 1954 and launched his own gubernatorial bid. It was a landmark campaign, the first time in the 20th century that the *Sun* had endorsed the Republican candidate for governor. With 700,000 casting ballots, McKeldin won by more than 60,000 votes. In an otherwise typical Maryland election that favored Democrats in most offices, according to Callcott, Byrd was dragged down by the aftermath of an ugly primary fight, which in time would carry a curious twist.

In 1966, George P. Mahoney won the state's Democratic gubernatorial primary, but his anticrime platform that declared, "Your home is your castle. Protect it" was attacked as subtly racist in contrast to the more moderate views of the Republican candidate. Baltimore County Executive Spiro T. Agnew won that election, but he wasn't in the governor's mansion long, as Richard M. Nixon tabbed him to be his running mate in the 1968 presidential election. Agnew resigned after an investigation into an alleged bribery scheme, but he remains the only Marylander ever to be a heartbeat from the Oval Office.

Mahoney had been on the other side of the race card in 1954, when he challenged Byrd in the Democratic primary. His attacks on Byrd included reports of lax academic standards for Terp athletes and the university's history of segregation. Byrd had a Pyrrhic victory. The primary split the party and left him with a winning margin of just 4,000 votes, and he never found his stride in the general election. Callcott wrote that when his son William graduated from Maryland in the arena that Byrd had planned, Governor McKeldin and President Wilson H. Elkins alluded to the university's new respectability on academic fronts. As Byrd paced on the concourse, his name was never mentioned.

A month to the day after the arena opened with the win over Virginia, Tatum coached his last football game at Maryland, as the unbeaten Terps lost 20-6 to Oklahoma in an Orange Bowl that amounted to the national championship game. Tatum resigned as coach and athletic director and jumped to the University of North Carolina. He cited a desire to work at his alma mater, but scrutiny and condemnation of the athletic buildup he had overseen were factors in his move. In the wake of the great college basketball-fixing scandal of 1951, a New York judge had cited Maryland as one of the universities that had turned football into a commercial enterprise. Byrd's 1954 gubernatorial campaign had been embarrassed when a critical evaluation from the Middle States Association of Colleges and Secondary Schools had been made public. It damned admissions policies for football players and the snail's pace at which they progressed toward degrees.

Maryland began a gradual deemphasis of big-time athletics, and it wouldn't get back into that game until 1969, when longtime track and field coach Jim Kehoe was made athletic director and the Terps rejoined the arms—and legs—race in football and basketball. In the interim, the Terps performed in a half-empty Cole on too many winter nights in the late 1950s and for much of the 1960s.

"You ever heard of Seward's Folly?" Kehoe asked, referring to the 19th-century purchase of barren lands that would become Alaska. "Curley building Cole was ridiculed. I always viewed Curley as a man of great vision, someone who thought 10, 20, 30 years ahead of the current time, but the *Baltimore Sun* and a lot of people said there was no need for it. There was no way an arena of that size could ever be needed or used. It was a disaster when it was built, yet it turned out to be a great thing."

3

JOHNNY UNITAS was the central figure of a seminal moment in American professional sports, the National Football League (NFL) championship game between the Baltimore Colts and the New York Giants in 1958, when the college game enjoyed greater popularity than the NFL. The game came to be called "the greatest ever played," but it was rather ordinary until Unitas delivered the stuff of a classic. He drove the Colts 73 yards at the end of regulation to force a tie and then 80 yards in overtime for a 23-17 victory.

A master of the two-minute drill before John Elway was even born, Unitas was all of 25 years old when he directed Baltimore to its first NFL championship. He would have fit right in with the 1957–58 Terps, who leaned on the discipline and experience that several men in their mid-20s had picked up during military duty to become the only Maryland team before 1973 to reach the NCAA tournament.

Unitas was born on May 7, 1933, eight months after Terp guard Tom Young, another gritty product of western Pennsylvania. John Nacincik, a 6-foot-3 forward, was born the same year as Unitas. When Bud Millikan gathered the Terps in the autumn of 1957, Young had already celebrated his 25th birthday. Young, Nacincik, and reserve big man Perry Moore stood out as men among teenage boys, service veterans who were settling down and starting families.

Gary Williams and other modern coaches recruit high school talent with the NBA draft in mind. Is a prospect better than my program? Will a Chris Wilcox use us as a halfway house for a season or two, then bolt for the pros? If he does, will we have someone ready to step in and start?

Millikan worried about inquiries from Uncle Sam, not the NBA, but the GI Bill benefited coaches, too. While some of their younger teammates would cower from the unrelenting demands of Millikan, the veterans had experienced the regimen of drill instructors and the rhythms of the military. Besides, after road games they could join trainer Duke Wyre and cool down with a legal beer.

"Nacincik, Moore, and myself, we were all married and veterans of the armed services," Young said. "We were older and more mature, and that helped us."

OFFICIAL
PROGRAM
35¢

FEBRUARY 13, 1958

MARYLAND
vs
CLEMSON

STUDENT ACTIVITIES BUILDING
COLLEGE PARK,
MARYLAND

Everything was cheaper in 1958, when fans watched a Maryland team that would earn the program's first berth in the NCAA tournament. (Maryland Sports Information.)

Young experienced Maryland basketball both at Ritchie Coliseum and in the Southern Conference, as he had played with Gene Shue and received his first varsity letters in 1952–53 and 1953–54. He was from Natrona Heights, Pennsylvania, the origin of a pipeline of football talent that fueled the growth that brought the Terps a national championship in 1953. To this day, Young would rather watch an NFL game than college basketball, and in high school he had wanted to be like the heroes from his hometown, Ed and Dick Modzelewski. "Big Mo" and "Little Mo" had helped Jim Tatum put Maryland on the football map, but "Skinny" Young had weighed 151 pounds coming out of high school, so he had stuck to hoops.

Young would have concluded his Maryland career the season before Cole Field House opened had he not received, in December 1953, the army induction notice that led him to say so long to his basketball team-mates and prepare to withdraw from Maryland. Young said that friends in high places, however, pulled strings that allowed him to complete his junior season with the Terps.

"I had already received my induction notice by the time we went to play at West Virginia," Young said. "After the game, I left Morgantown and went home with my parents, because I had to leave the following week. I was home two days, when I was notified that my draft had been put on hold and would be delayed until the summer. I was able to finish my junior year, and I maybe missed one game. I believe Jim Tatum had more to do with that than anyone."

Young spent an easy 19 months on a base outside Frankfurt, Germany, but getting to Europe was an ordeal. He shipped out of New York Harbor on a troop transport on New Year's Day, 1955.

"I spent the worst seven days of my life on that boat," Young said. "This was in the days of the Iron Curtain, and I was assigned to a Military Intelligence group. They would bring in men who were thought to be spies, and interrogate them. I was supposed to be a clerk typist, but I was put on TDY [temporary duty] the whole time, and played ball. The colonel in charge happened to like sports a great deal, and I was assigned to the gymnasium. It was good duty, almost like being on a college campus. I fol-lowed Maryland very closely while I was away, but it wasn't easy. *Stars and Stripes* had the scores a day or two late. It wasn't like watching CNN."

Nacincik learned about the University of Maryland while he was sta-tioned at the Anacostia Naval Receiving Station. He had enlisted in the navy in May 1952, after he had dropped out of high school in Brooklyn, New York. Raised in the Williamsburg section of the borough, Nacincik had never gotten to play high school basketball. Extracurricular activities had been canceled by a teachers' job action, so he learned basketball playing pick-up at Far Rockaway Beach. His acquaintances included Sherman White, who would serve eight months in prison for his role in the point-shaving scandal that would lead Long Island University to deemphasize the sport and Kentucky's Adolph Rupp to regret a state-ment that fixers couldn't touch his boys "with a ten-foot pole."

"When you're born and raised in the city, the only thing you play is basketball," Nacincik said. "There was no room for anything else."

Young's return coincided with the arrival on the varsity of two long, lean sophomores from New Jersey, 6-9 Al Bunge and 6-6 Charlie McNeil. Nacincik, Nick Davis, and Perry Moore were seniors who two seasons earlier had played in the first game at Cole. All of that experience on the perimeter, combined with the worldly ways and military discipline of the veterans, led Millikan to loosen the reins a little. Iba had taught him the value of a patterned offense and staunch man-to-man defense, but Millikan's Terps reached a new scoring high by averaging 69.1 points in 1957–58.

"It wasn't up-tempo, and we never pressed," Young said, "but there's no doubt that Bud let that team run with the ball more than any other he'd had to that point."

Jerry Bechtle spent the 1956–57 season on the freshman team with Bunge and McNeil, and he found a different attitude when he moved up to the varsity.

"In the case of Nacincik, Young, and Moore, they were much more mature than the rest of us," Bechtle said. "Those guys gravitated to Millikan, and he respected them. Bud respected that maturity, it helped them handle his demands. That was the nice thing about a mature bunch of guys, they could play well in the Bud Millikan system."

The highlight of the school year occurred on October 19. During a visit to the United States, Queen Elizabeth took a day to sample America's sporting culture and watched the Terps football team beat North Carolina 21-7 at Byrd Stadium. In nearby Cole, Millikan thought he might have the makings of something regal of his own. Young and the sophomores joined a group of holdovers who had finished second to North Carolina in the ACC in 1956–57. That Tar Heel team had capped a 32-0 season by knocking off Kansas and Wilt Chamberlain in a triple-overtime NCAA final.

With ACC Player of the Year Lennie Rosenbluth gone to the NBA and center Joe Quigg out all season with an injury, North Carolina fell back to the pack in 1957–58, but the Tar Heels still had only one loss when they came to Cole on January 11. North Carolina had fallen to No. 1 West Virginia and Jerry West by 11 points in the Kentucky Invitational, but Maryland's 74-61 victory over the Tar Heels was an accomplishment to savor. So was a December 9 win at Cole over Kentucky, as Rupp made a second trip to the showcase arena in College Park.

There was no powerhouse team in the ACC, and even after a lost weekend at North Carolina and Duke in February, Maryland's fourth-place

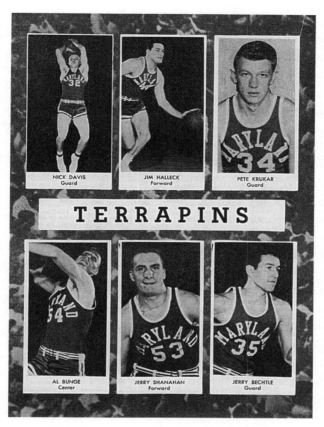

TERRAPINS

NICK DAVIS
Guard

JIM HALLECK
Forward

PETE KRUKAR
Guard

AL BUNGE
Center

JERRY SHANAHAN
Forward

JERRY BECHTLE
Guard

The Terps had a balanced bunch during the 1957–58 season, when sophomore Al Bunge (lower left) was their top rebounder and third-leading scorer despite being weakened by ulcerative colitis. (Maryland Sports Information.)

finish of 9-5 left them just two games behind the regular-season champion Blue Devils, who went 11-3. Through 1966, the conference tournament was held in Reynolds Coliseum, the home of North Carolina State, and the Terps were not paid much notice when they arrived in Raleigh.

Davis and McNeil combined for 46 points in a 70-66 first-round win over Virginia. Davis went for another 22 in the semifinals, when Maryland upset top-seeded and sixth-ranked Duke, 71-65. After that overtime ordeal, the championship game seemed easy, even after the Terps fell behind No. 13 North Carolina 34-27 at the break.

"I bet you the game wasn't a minute and a half old when I catch a technical," Millikan said. "The benches were at the end of the floor in those days. I jumped off ours and walked down in front of my players. I was not complaining to the floor, I just wanted to make a point to some of my players."

Maryland exploded for 59 points in the second half for an 86-74 victory and the university's first berth in the NCAA tournament. It was the only instance in the first 17 ACC tournaments in which an interloper from outside the state of North Carolina ruled.

"That whole ACC tournament, there was not one time when we didn't feel good as a team," Young said. "North Carolina had dominated us the year before, but we had beaten them at our place. We felt we could beat anyone down there, especially on a neutral court. McNeil and Davis usually did the bulk of our scoring, but Bill Murphy was the man against North Carolina in the championship game. He had a great game off the bench. He could shoot it, and shoot it anytime."

Murphy was actually an afterthought in Millikan's rotation. The 6-foot-3 junior from Pittsburgh hadn't scored in the semifinals against Duke, but Millikan needed another shooter to chip into that halftime deficit, and Murphy rewarded his hunch with a career game in the final. McNeil scored a team-high 21 points against North Carolina and joined tournament MVP Davis on the all-tournament team, but Murphy's 19 were cited as the difference. He had contributed just 35 points in Maryland's other 28 games, and his final average for the season was 2.7 points.

Millikan celebrated for about three minutes before he began to think about the NCAA tournament. Despite North Carolina's 1957 title, the ACC was not highly regarded, and its champion did not warrant one of the eight first-round byes in the 24-team NCAA tournament. The Terps hustled back to campus and then immediately on to Madison Square Garden, where they had to play Boston College just three days after the ACC final. Davis came out on fire, and Maryland cruised to an 86-63 win and a spot in the Sweet 16.

The ACC tournament had vaulted Maryland to No. 6 in the national rankings, and the Terps viewed themselves as legitimate contenders for the NCAA crown, despite a field toughened by the most remarkable collection of talent that college basketball had ever seen. Conferences like the ACC and colleges like Maryland practiced segregation, but African Americans assumed a place of prominence elsewhere. Seattle and its Elgin Baylor, a product of Spingarn High in Washington, D.C., loomed out west. Maryland was in the other half of the draw, along with Cincinnati and its incredible sophomore, Oscar Robertson. The Terps' win over North Carolina meant the NCAA tournament was without a defending champion. Kansas and Chamberlain were also absent, as Kansas State had taken the Big Eight Conference behind Bob Boozer and coach Tex Winter, the inventor of a triangle offense that would figure in Michael Jordan's six NBA titles. Kentucky was favored in the Mideast, but Maryland had beaten Rupp's dynasty back on December 9.

More than four decades later, some of Millikan's men think that Temple would not have eliminated them in the Charlotte Coliseum on March 14 if Bunge's physical woes hadn't flared up.

Bunge jokes that his most memorable moment with Maryland came at Kentucky in December 1958, when his foul led to a three-point play that forced an overtime and snatched victory away from the Terps. He neglects to mention that he was the only Maryland player between Gene Shue in 1954 and Tom McMillen in 1972 to be voted first-team all-ACC. Bunge's resume in 1960 included a 43-point game against Yale that would stand as the Terp scoring record for 18 years.

"Bunge was never a superstar, but other than Gene Shue, he was head and shoulders above everyone else from that era," classmate Bechtle said. "He was another Jersey guy, a superb athlete who was all-state in football and baseball. Al was an average shooter who blended well into Millikan's system, but he was always playing through physical problems."

As a sophomore in 1957–58, Bunge led Maryland in rebounds with 9.1 a game and was third in scoring, but he rarely felt fit. Millikan put a foot down about Ledo's Restaurant gift certificates that were given to the top scorer and rebounder from each game, but Bunge needed the grub. His playing weight was listed as 215 pounds, but he was less than 200 after dealing with Millikan's practices, which during semester break ran to three a day.

"I had ulcerative colitis," Bunge said. "The first day of practice, I couldn't even run down the floor. Eventually, I got into shape, but the colitis came back. I just couldn't run very long. Bud would put me in the game, but then I would have to come right back out. I missed my finals in May because I was rushed to University Hospital in Baltimore. When the NCAA tournament rolled around, I was about 20, 25 pounds underweight. I think we would've beaten Temple if I'd been healthy. I think Patton was the name of the tank I ran into."

Guy Rodgers averaged better than 20 points, and Bill "Pickles" Kennedy was another steady player on the perimeter for Temple, but Tink Van Patton's physical play left an impression on Bunge.

"At that time, you didn't have national officials," Young said. "There were different brands of basketball around the country. The Big Ten was much more aggressive than the ACC, where they would call touch fouls. To us, the Big Ten was almost like playing football. Temple was like that, huge inside and very physical. I'm certain we had Big Ten officials, and we weren't used to that. Even with that, the game still went down to the last minute. We were down one, called a time-out, and had a play called for Charlie McNeil."

There was confusion coming out of the break, and McNeil never got off a shot, as Kennedy's steal sealed a 71-67 win for Temple. A day later, the Owls handled Dartmouth in the East regional final. The following weekend, Temple played Kentucky in the NCAA semifinals in Louisville, which at the time was about as fair as taking on the Russians in Moscow. Kentucky beat Temple by 1 and Seattle by 12 to take the last of Rupp's four NCAA championships.

Maryland beat Manhattan in the East consolation game to conclude a 22-7 season that produced what would be the first of many NCAA opportunities for the Terps. Maryland would lament them all until its 19th spin at the Big Dance.

4

BUD MILLIKAN WAS UNABLE to parlay the trip to the 1958 NCAA tournament into a recruiting bonanza, and the administration's laissez-faire approach to big-time basketball and football led to a series of forgettable winters at Cole. Four of the next six seasons produced losing records, and only once in that stretch did the Terps advance beyond the first round of the ACC tournament. There was a third-place regular-season finish in 1959–60, but Maryland lost its tournament opener to host N.C. State. Declining attendance led the ACC to suspend regional TV coverage that year, and Al Bunge's stellar senior season got little notice beyond an invitation to the U.S. Olympic trials and a semipro contract with the Phillips 66ers.

If Cole was quiet in December, January, and February, it came to life in March. The Maryland Public Secondary Schools Athletic Association (MPSSAA), which governed sports at public high schools in the 23 counties, jumped at the chance to stage its championships in College Park, and Cole became the site of its semifinals and finals in 1956. The climactic weekend of the MPSSAA tournament became a fixture at Cole, but the biggest high school game ever staged there matched a pair of Catholic schools, DeMatha of nearby Hyattsville and New York's Power Memorial, whose team included a budding legend who would go on to set the NBA career scoring record.

In his pre-Muslim days, Kareem Abdul-Jabbar was known as Lew Alcindor, and in 1965 Power Memorial played its second game in as many seasons against DeMatha at Cole. It sold out three weeks in advance, and scalpers got $50 for a ticket, ten times the cost of a prime seat at an NBA game. With correspondents from *Time* and *Newsweek* at Cole, Alcindor suffered the only loss of his prep career, and the ascendance of Morgan Wootten's DeMatha program to the center of the high school universe accelerated.

Cole could be a cavernous setting for Maryland-Clemson and high school games that involved teams with no following, but the NCAA needed an East Coast venue, and 1964 was the only March from 1962 to 1970 that passed without a visit from the national tournament. ACC

Player of the Year Len Chappell and Billy Packer, now a CBS analyst, led Wake Forest to the Eastern Regional title there in 1962. The ACC was still lightly regarded, and Wake Forest had to go to the Palestra in Philadelphia and beat Yale to advance to the East's Sweet 16 and play in the first NCAA tournament game at Cole.

Coach Horace "Bones" McKinney's Demon Deacons beat St. Joseph's, 96-85, in overtime, then took Villanova, 79-69, to earn the only Final Four berth in Wake Forest history. Wake lost in the NCAA semifinals to Ohio State, and only one team—Maryland—gave the Demon Deacons a worse beating that season. The Buckeyes whipped Wake Forest by 22 in early December, but the Demon Deacons were still ranked No. 3 a week later, when they were beaten by the Terps, 79-62.

"I have a great memory of my last game at Cole, as opposed to what could have been my last game there," Packer said. "After we lost at Maryland, I can remember sitting back on the same parking lot that I've walked in through a hundred times to call games, tears rolling down my face. We knew the ACC champ was going to play in Cole, if it could get through the play-in game. St. Joe's had beat us the year before in the regional final, and there was a real good rivalry between Bones and Jack Ramsay [the St. Joseph's coach]. I know a Wake booster brought a dead chicken to use as a prop when we finally beat the Hawks. As the game was winding down, he threw it on the floor. They missed a big free throw, and we won rather handily in overtime. They had fans and the press down on the floor for the NCAAs, but in the regular season Cole was a sterile environment."

Maryland's victims at Cole in the 1961–62 season included North Carolina, which lost by the identical score that took down Wake Forest, 79-62. In the first of his 36 seasons at Chapel Hill, Dean Smith was in the midst of a four-game losing streak that produced his only losing record. In 2002, Smith joshed, "I thought I should have gotten out of coaching" after that loss, but Cole would become one of his favorite courts. He went 30-12 at Cole, and he compiled more wins there than Bob Wade did in his three seasons as the Terps' head coach. Smith was 6-0 in NCAA tournament games at Cole, as he used College Park to get to the Final Four in 1967, 1969, and 1977.

Presidential candidate-to-be Bill Bradley set a slew of NCAA tournament scoring records for Princeton in 1965, when he was a perfect 29-for-29 at the free-throw line in Eastern Regional wins at Cole over N.C. State and Providence.

In the 1990s, the NCAA adopted a 30,000-seat minimum for the Final Four, which put the tournament's climax in domed football stadiums and cemented Cole's status as the only on-campus arena to house two Final Fours. The 1966 and 1970 tournaments were bookends to the three titles won by UCLA during the Alcindor era. UCLA and Sidney Wicks stared down Jacksonville and Artis Gilmore in a 1970 finale that didn't match its hype, but all the 1966 championship game delivered was one of the weightiest confrontations in the history of college basketball.

That final would be labeled college basketball's *Brown vs. Board of Education*, a reference to a landmark 1954 case in which the Supreme Court had banned segregation in public schools. The game had implications for African American athletes, and it was made all the more poignant by the presence in Cole of a Maryland trailblazer. When Texas Western took down Kentucky, it was in a unique NCAA championship game, as the former started five blacks and used two more men of color off the bench to beat an all-white squad coached by a legend whose legacy was stained by racism. The lore that grew out of the 1966 NCAA final held that there were no blacks in the major southern conferences, but in fact the ACC included a minority player, and Maryland sophomore Billy Jones sat a few rows behind the Kentucky bench, entertaining a Terp recruit. Jones appeared in just 16 games for Maryland that season, but his impact went beyond averages of 2.8 points and 2.0 rebounds.

Maryland had suited up Darryl Hill, the ACC's first black football player, in 1963. Earlier that year, as part of Maryland's junior recruiting, Millikan had literally walked out of his office to watch a state tournament that included Jones, Fairmont Heights' Pete Johnson, and Cambridge's Dick Drescher. Football was Jones's favorite sport, but Baltimore County Executive Spiro T. Agnew hadn't yet gotten that added to the interscholastic sports program, so he had gravitated to basketball and lacrosse at Towson High. Jones led the Generals to the Class AA state championship by putting up 58 points in wins over Walter Johnson and Bladensburg. The title was an anomaly, one of only two boys' championships produced by Baltimore County between 1948 and 1988. Towson was unable to repeat in 1964, when Jones scored an MPSSAA semifinal record of 41 points in an overtime win over Surrattsville but was outmanned in a championship game loss to Allegany. By then, Millikan had already recognized a distinctive talent, a young man with the strength to venture where no other blacks had gone.

"It really wasn't all that bad," Millikan said in 2001 of his decision to take his recruiting into the black enclave of East Towson. "You put on a red uniform and go in to play at Chapel Hill, and you're not going to be looked on with any favor anyway. My thinking was, he's a fine young man, he needs an education, and he can play basketball. Billy had a

Billy Jones broke the color barrier in the Atlantic Coast Conference. During the 1965–66 season, he became the first African American to play varsity basketball in the ACC. (Hornbake Library.)

wonderful mother. They lived in a small house, had one of those old-time, pot-bellied kerosene stoves that burned your eyes."

Jones's ears would burn at times over the next four years.

In 1963, the Maryland recruiting class included Joe Harrington, Jay McMillen, and a scrawny point guard from New Jersey named Gary Williams. Jones and Pete Johnson, another African American, arrived on campus in September 1964, and after they spent a season on the freshman team, Johnson was held back because of academics and Jones made history. Ali Khan, then known as Chris Richmond, played for Anacostia High in Washington, D.C., and attended a junior college in California and Arizona State before he transferred to Maryland. He practiced with the Terps during the 1964–65 season, but there is no record of his appearing in a game, so Jones was the one who broke the color barrier in the ACC. There was an uneasy encounter over the segregated policies of one dining room down South, but the reception of Jones at the ACC tournament was a bit warmer. When he came off the bench and entered a first-round game against North Carolina on March 3, 1966, there was polite applause at Reynolds Coliseum.

"Some basketball people appreciated what I was doing," said Jones, who shot a poor 1-for-8 against the Tar Heels that day, in a 1999 interview for the *Sun*. "You've got to remember, South Carolina had a bunch of players from New York, and they were used to dealing with people like me. I do remember one instance at South Carolina, when I was going for a ball rolling into the corner, and somebody in the stands called me a nigger. That was the exception. I don't remember any issues when we traveled. I was not the most sophisticated kid, but Gary Ward and the guys made sure I was taken care of. In America in 1966, you had to be smart, always cognizant of where you were. I received better treatment in the ACC than I did in my home county. I remember playing lacrosse for Towson, and someone putting their stick in my groin with the intent to injure. We had an upset win in basketball at Dundalk. The crowd rocked our bus as we were trying to get off the parking lot."

There were approximately 200 blacks on campus when Jones came to College Park.

"Society on the College Park campus was no different than anywhere else," Jones said. "As much as possible, we did things together, but Gary Williams and the rest of the guys were welcome in places where I was not. You're captain of the basketball team as a senior, and you get no offers to join a fraternity? I understood. I wasn't even irritated."

Jones shrugged off the vestiges of racism that left an impression on his teammates, and exposed them to his world. McMillen, who'd been raised on Top 40 radio and taken piano lessons until he was a high school senior in Mansfield, Pennsylvania, said that black music "was a revelation." Williams got a feel for being a minority when Jones took him to a rhythm and blues show at the Howard Theater on Florida Avenue in Washington, D.C.

"There was a big rumor that the Temptations were going to be there," Williams said. "It was an experience I'll never forget. The Temps didn't show, but there were eight other acts. You never thought about Billy's situation, 'What's it like being the only black guy on the team?' but you walked into that theater, looked around and said, 'Wow.' One thing that shook us up came after we played at Duke. We went from the gym to the train station in Durham. There was a line where blacks ordered food, and another for whites. That was the first time I had ever seen that. Not that we were heroes, but we all left. Billy Jones never got the credit he deserved, because when Dean Smith retired, everyone made it seem like he broke the [ACC] racial barrier with Charlie Scott. Billy might have been the first black person in the South Carolina and Clemson gyms who wasn't sweeping the floor."

Maryland is the northern outpost in the ACC, but the Ku Klux Klan was alive and well in scattered pockets of the state, and Jim Crow practices received tacit approval. A prominent Charles County landowner was found guilty of manslaughter for beating a Baltimore barmaid with his cane after she allegedly delivered his drink too slowly in 1963, and he was sentenced to six months in jail and a fine of $500. It wasn't until 1967 that the federal government approved desegregation plans that would eliminate all-black schools in four Maryland counties. When the Final Four first came to Cole, there was an all-black high school, Bates, a short walk from the state capitol building in Annapolis. During that 1965–66 school year, the freshman class at all-black George Washington Carver High in St. Mary's County included Tubby Smith, who would call the shots as the coach of Kentucky's 1998 NCAA championship team.

The Final Four was such a small-potatoes event in 1966 that Maryland officials began the school year not even knowing it was coming their way.

"The M Club had put on a number of exhibitions at Cole," booster Jack Heise said. "Red Auerbach brought the Celtics in for an exhibition every year, and the Harlem Globetrotters would stop on their tours. We were used to having big events. Chicago was supposed to have the 1966 Final Four, but when the ticket takers and security people there went on strike, we got it. We only had a couple of months of lag time to get the thing organized. Our volunteer group worked everything out."

The championship weekend wasn't even known as the Final Four, and without a day between the semifinals and the final for rest and hype, it was not yet a big media event. The UCLA freshmen, with Alcindor, might

Billy Jones (30) was welcomed by his teammates and Bud Millikan, yet he dealt with isolation not just in the ACC, but also in College Park. (Hornbake Library.)

have been the best team in the nation. Another rookie of note was Bob Knight, the first-year coach at Army.

Kentucky disposed of Duke, which had ACC Player of the Year Steve Vacendak and Jack Marin, and Texas Western beat Utah and Jerry Chambers in the other semifinal on Friday, March 18. The winners came right back the next day and turned some stereotypes on their head.

Two days after Texas Western surprised Kentucky, 72-65, to win the NCAA title, the *Lexington Herald* editorialized: "There is no disgrace in losing to a team such as was assembled by Texas Western after a nation-wide search for talent that somehow escaped the recruiters for the Globe Trotters." Yes, Miner coach Don Haskins had brought big-city talent to remote El Paso, but Kentucky's All-Americans, Pat Riley and Louie Dampier, hailed from Schenectady, N.Y., and Indianapolis, respectively. "Rupp's Runts" didn't have a starter over 6-5, but they played run-and-gun and set a school scoring record with 86.9 points a game. While Rupp pushed the pace, Haskins, like Millikan, was a disciple of Henry Iba's, and the Miners were among the nation's defensive leaders. They allowed only 62.7 points a game, and any guard fortunate to get past Bobby Joe Hill was funneled to defensive stopper David Lattin.

"The thing that sticks out in my mind is the tremendous defensive ability of Texas Western," said Larry Conley, a Kentucky starter who became an ESPN analyst. "They took us completely out of our game. I can remember to this day the frustration I felt at the half, over how they had taken us out of our game."

Baltimore native Frank Deford reported on the game for *Sports Illustrated*. A few weeks earlier, his cover story had portrayed a mellowing Rupp, and he was granted access to the Kentucky locker room at halftime.

"Rupp said I could only write about it if Kentucky won," Deford told the *Sun* in 1999. "Lattin was very strong, built like Charles Barkley. Rupp said to Cliff Berger something to the effect, 'if you can stop that big coon.' . . . I never talked about it until years later, after he [Rupp] died."

Deford is among those who think the 1966 final has been blown out of proportion. San Francisco and Bill Russell had ruled college basketball in 1955 and 1956. The consensus All-America team in 1958 had consisted of five African Americans. Cincinnati and Loyola of Chicago had started four blacks when they won NCAA titles in 1962 and 1963, respectively. Texas Western won in ACC country, however, where segregation was one reason that the conference had produced just one NCAA finalist in its first decade, the 1957 champions from North Carolina.

"From a historical perspective, I didn't realize what I was watching when Kentucky played Texas Western," Jones said. "I can remember Texas

Western reminding me of how we played back home. It was the city game. There was a sense of pride in watching those guys play. They reminded me of the guys back home."

Most of Jones's friends back in Baltimore and Towson were restricted to opportunities at historically black colleges that today make up the Mid-Eastern Athletic Conference and the Central Intercollegiate Athletic Association. Jones, meanwhile, continued to prosper at Maryland. He averaged 11.6 points and 5.0 rebounds as a junior, 10.2 points and 5.6 rebounds as a senior captain in 1967–68. Johnson was the Terps' leading scorer that season.

What about Rupp? He retired in 1972 and died five years later. "The Baron" continues to be one of college basketball's bogeymen, but he wasn't the last coach to take an all-white team to the Final Four. The next year, with Scott on its freshman team, North Carolina emerged from the Eastern Regional at Cole, and Smith took an all-white team to the 1967 Final Four.

It was played in Kentucky.

FOR TWO GLORIOUS DAYS in New Orleans, it appeared that Maryland had the makings of a team that could advance to the 1966 NCAA tournament that climaxed at Cole Field House, but the Terps returned to their customary form and finished in the middle of the ACC pack. Within 15 months Millikan was gone, out of coaching at age 46.

When Maryland won the Sugar Bowl Tournament in December 1965, its players could be excused for fanciful dreams that they might be able to participate in the Final Four that was to be held on their own floor in three months. On successive nights, they beat Houston and sophomore Elvin Hayes, 69-68, in the semifinals, then defeated Dayton and "High" Henry Finkel, 77-75, in the championship game to claim the Terps' first tournament title of any kind since the 1958 ACC championship. Both Houston and Dayton reached the Sweet 16 that season, and they went to the Final Four the following year.

"I tell my friends I held Elvin Hayes to 28 and Henry Finkel to 44," Jay McMillen said. "I was a center, and that was part of our problem."

The 6-7 McMillen was part of a junior class that included Gary Williams and Joe Harrington. The seniors were Gary Ward, Neil Brayton, and Rick Wise, and Billy Jones headed the sophomore class. There was some talent, but not enough to overcome a knee injury to Harrington, the dwindling focus of some of his teammates, and the administration's lack of desire to push the major sports. Any momentum was left behind in the Big Easy, as the Terps followed their Sugar Bowl Tournament title with four straight losses in the ACC.

"There weren't 50 preseason rankings like there are now," Williams said. "*Sports Illustrated* was the big ranking, and they had us 12th going into my junior year. We thought we had a chance to be really good, because we returned everyone from a team that had tied for second in the ACC. We won that tournament in New Orleans, and told ourselves, 'We're really good.' We came home, practiced for a couple of days, then went to Carolina and got our socks blown off. Guys lost interest in basketball. We had something like five guys join fraternities, which were a big deal. Bud used to have this expression, 'Down the House.' He blamed that on the way we played in the second half of the year."

Thinking that it hastened recovery time, Bud Millikan had his players lie on their stomachs during time-outs. It didn't help in this 1958 loss to N.C. State at Cole, but Millikan enjoyed his finest hour two months later, when Maryland won its first ACC championship. (Hornbake Library.)

McMillen didn't notice Millikan fretting about the influence of fraternities, but he does grant Williams a point or two. "College basketball wasn't a business like it is today," McMillen said. "If I was going to be on ESPN three nights a week and have Dick Vitale raving about me, I would have spent more time on basketball. We were supposed to go to class, and we were supposed to get a degree. It's not even an issue today; basketball is primo. When you're on TV three nights a week, you know where your value is. I'm not sure now is better. Life is getting a degree, getting a job, having a family, and not being catered to like you're a rock star. That said, we had a bunch of screw-ups, and Gary's right, we could have done better. He was everything Bud wanted in a player. He never went out, never partied, didn't screw around. He was dedicated and wanted to win, but he was in the minority. It took him 15 years longer than the rest of us to open up to sin and corruption. Gary was the Ayatollah, in wanting to win."

McMillen's sarcasm aside, the Terps might have been big men on campus, but minus constant television coverage, they remained private figures. Over semester break, they lived in Cole, in housing quarters two floors above the office where Williams would one day plot Maryland's way to an NCAA title. Theirs were the days of "Animal House," and their semester-break traditions included road trips to "the Block," Baltimore's red-light district. Ogling the strippers and heckling the comics, they weren't celebrities, just taller than normal college knuckleheads. The morning after one season ended with their customary elimination from the ACC tournament, they awoke and headed down to the training table, where one of the trainers had placed a Budweiser at each setting.

While nearly all of Williams's modern Terps are deluded into thinking that they have a future in the NBA, Millikan's comprehended that for most, the only way to remain in basketball was through coaching. Harrington would be an assistant at Maryland until the mid-1970s, then head up Hofstra, George Mason, Long Beach State, and Colorado. Starting nearly from scratch, Jones turned the University of Maryland Baltimore County into a Division II regional power from 1974 to 1986. Terry Truax, who said that the population of his residence hall was greater than that of his home-town of Hancock, took Towson State University to its only two NCAA tournaments, in 1990 and 1991. From an earlier vintage, Tom Young took Rutgers to the Final Four in 1976. Look back further for Millikan pupils, and you'll find Shue, who worked the NBA finals twice; Morgan Wootten, a student at Maryland before he built his dynasty at DeMatha; and dozens of other college and high school coaches.

"I was a physical education major, and I took Bud's basketball class in the 1953–54 school year," Wootten said. "It was held in Ritchie, with practical demonstrations that showed you how to teach a particular skill. We spent a lot of time in the classroom, too, talking about philosophy and execution. I don't think that a better Xs and Os guy ever lived."

Millikan wanted his players to dress a certain way and play a certain way. "Dean Smith got credit for having a system, but Bud had a system before it was fashionable," Truax said. "His attention to detail was thorough. There's an old saying that it's not what you coach, it's what you emphasize. With Bud, you played defense, you went to class, you dressed a certain way, you looked a certain way. It was an excellent training ground for guys who wanted to go into coaching. A lot of other coaches produced greater numbers, but some of that has to do with name recognition. No disrespect to Digger Phelps, but his assistants weren't hired because of the training they received but because of the Notre Dame name. If you played for Coach Millikan, it was like eight semesters of basketball theory."

The Millikan branch was one of many that grew out of Henry Iba's family tree. There is the Eddie Sutton line, which influenced coaches like Gene Keady and Rob Evans. Before Don Haskins won an NCAA title for Texas Western in 1966, his players included Nolan Richardson, who guided Arkansas to an NCAA championship in 1994. All that success can be traced to the fundamentals preached by Iba, which Millikan tweaked with his military training. Stations—moving from different drills to perfect different skills—wasn't just the inspiration of a coach.

"There was open-square instruction in the military, and that's the way I coached football, too," said Millikan, who was an assistant football coach one year at Oklahoma State. "A group here, a group there, blow the whistle, and rotate. My first day at Maryland, I blew the whistle, every guy got one last shot in and then came over while the manager I had inherited went chasing every direction after the balls. I said, 'Gentlemen, everyone who had a ball when I blew the whistle, go get one and put it in the box.' They looked at me funny, but from then on we had discipline on the floor. When I blow that whistle during practice, I want them to stop in their tracks so we can find out what we did wrong and what we're supposed to do."

That would be to take care of the basketball. "He really valued the ball," Young said, "and coming out of high school, that wasn't something I had learned to the degree he stressed at Maryland."

Drew Schaufler, among Maryland's starting five for the first game played at Cole, remembers Young throwing a cross-court pass into the stands at Ritchie and following the ball's path right to a seat at the end of the bench. He knew that Millikan was going to yank him.

"If we won 4-2, that was fine by Bud," Schaufler said. "You would score, and he would take you out. He was a difficult guy to play for. Everyone is still afraid of him. At reunions he still comes up to you and says, 'How do you do, son?' We say 'I'm all right, coach.' He always appeared to be older than he was. He was a very disciplined man, and he knew defense. He was a disciple of Iba, and he believed that that way of basketball was it. He couldn't stand throwing the ball away. Bob O'Brien and Nick Davis could handle the ball, and they thought they were as slick as Hot Rod Hundley. Bud got in O'Brien's face once and said, 'Son, you handle that ball like it's made out of snot.' Bud wanted you to play a certain way, and look a certain way. John Sandbower always had an intense look on his face; he looked like he was mad at the world. Bud loved that."

Even opponents bristled at Millikan's deliberate ways. In 1953, Wake Forest coach Murray Greason, explaining to Merrell Whittlesey of the *Washington Star* why he refused to schedule Maryland, said, "Why play a team that wants to walk?" Millikan loosened up in his second decade at Maryland and let the Terps run more. In 1964–65, they averaged 73.4 points, more than Maryland did in Lefty Driesell's last two seasons with the Terps, but toward the end of the Millikan era his ways seemed stodgy. The year he left Maryland, Lew Alcindor triggered the UCLA fast break and led the NCAA to take the drastic measure of outlawing the dunk, a prohibition that it wouldn't lift until 1976. Pete Maravich was a freshman at Louisiana State University, and about to light up the scoreboard.

It's telling that most of the coaches who played for Millikan or assisted him became known for their up-tempo styles. The genesis of Williams's pressing, running philosophy lay in his first high school job, when he inherited an undersized team at Woodrow Wilson High in Camden, N.J., and realized he would get crushed in a half-court game. When Young took Rutgers to the Final Four, the Scarlet Knights finished fourth in the nation in scoring. Truax thrived at Towson by allowing his guards considerable freedom.

"I never second-guessed Bud's style, but in retrospect that's not the way I liked to play or coach," Truax said. "Gary [Williams] and I used to talk about that a lot. He said, 'My guys couldn't last one of Millikan's practices.' Gary wasn't talking about the physical conditioning; he meant the constant correcting and teaching. We would have a series of plays in practice. Bud would go back three previous plays to make a point. Guys wouldn't remember it, but his mind was like a projector that he could rewind. We did a lot of half-court work. We were allowed to get up and down the court some, but I felt he stopped us too much. In my mind, you take the best from everyone and stay away from the things you don't enjoy. Bud wasn't negative, but based on my experience with Morgan Wootten and Dean Smith, you have to be more upbeat. When you constantly criticize, your players are going to lose their effectiveness."

Millikan could take an average athlete and turn him into a serviceable player, but extraordinary ones chafed under his restrictions. "Bud got 110 percent out of an ordinary John Doe," said Jerry Bechtle, who played for Millikan from 1957 to 1960. "He made you play to your ultimate, otherwise you didn't play. We didn't do the things kids do today. We had a lot of guys who could dunk, but nobody dared do it in a game. He was like Vince Lombardi with the Packers sweep, we're going to jam the ball down your throat. It didn't take a rocket scientist to figure out what we

Gary Williams showed off his defensive stance and some high socks before his junior season. He was one of Bud Millikan's favorite players, and he went on to become one of his most accomplished coaching pupils. (Hornbake Library.)

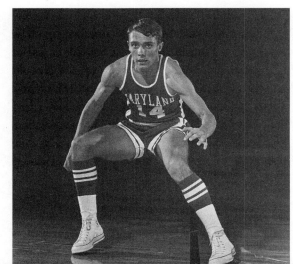

were doing. If you did anything contrary to the Millikan system, he blew the whistle and said, 'Where are you supposed to be?' If you had a lot of talent, it was tough fitting into his system."

Millikan didn't have the staff or recruiting budget of some of his Tobacco Road rivals, but he had something they didn't: Cole. Millikan disdained recruiting, but one visit to Cole was enough to sell most high school players. McMillen visited Indiana, Pittsburgh, St. Bonaventure, and Syracuse, but chose Maryland because Millikan was a decent man and Cole was the best arena he saw. Truax was sold on Maryland from the first time he played in the state tournament at Cole, in 1959. Billy Jones, Pete Johnson, and Dick Drescher all played in the state tournament at Cole in 1963. When Drescher led Cambridge High into the building, he said, "The place was so big, the baskets looked like Dixie cups."

Drescher, 6-4, was one of the undersized big men on Millikan's last team. Williams set a school record by making all eight of his field-goal attempts against South Carolina. Over the Christmas break, the Terps went to Charlotte, where Davidson coach Lefty Driesell took them lightly and scheduled Maryland as his semifinal patsy in a four-team invitational. The Terps upset Davidson in the semifinals, then beat Army, which had a stern sophomore named Mike Krzyzewski. Maryland was 11-8 overall and 5-4 in the ACC when it went into a skid and finished with six straight losses. It was the second longest losing streak of Millikan's tenure.

"Bud probably did his best coaching job that year," Williams said. "For most of the year we started three guys my size, Billy Jones, Pete Johnson, and myself. It was Joe Harrington when he was healthy, Jay McMillen, and Rich Drescher, basically all that played."

With the administration forcing his hand, Millikan called a team meeting to announce that he was resigning. Jones was student teaching and missed the announcement. Drescher, who in 1976 came within one place of representing the United States in the discus at the Montreal Olympics, was at track and field practice. In modern parlance, Millikan was "quired." He quit before he was fired, and took a job with a Maryland booster who wanted to expand his construction business and needed a man in Atlanta.

"I just decided I was going to get out of coaching," Millikan said. "I just didn't think I could live with it anymore. I didn't get the first sale I attempted to make, but it wasn't put in the paper the next day, what a horrible job I did. . . . I went into Maryland with this idea. I don't know if the people there are ever going to like me, but they're gonna respect me. The game of basketball is not the end; it has to carry over. I jokingly say I got out of it when we had to put hair dryers in the men's locker room. To me, it got to the point where you had to cheat to really win. We were not doing a good enough job with tuition, room and board, books, fees, and $15 a month. I felt you had to cheat academically or financially."

Millikan conducted himself in what he considered a dignified manner, and never had a hair out of place. Before coaching contracts included bonuses tied to graduation rates, his players got degrees. He won 243 games in his 17 seasons, the same number that Burt Shipley had piled up in 24. Millikan had 182 losses, and there were too many at the end for students who sought an escape on campus from the Vietnam War that was flaring up on the other side of the world. Like Smith at North Carolina, Millikan had been hung in effigy. He did not court the media, and wasn't about to pull any stunts to get attention, like some of the younger coaches he encountered.

Two years later, Maryland hired one of those brash young men. He didn't have much on his own head, but when Lefty Driesell came to College Park, the Terps let their hair down.

6

LATE IN THE 1960s, Davidson College head coach Lefty Driesell and Wake Forest assistant Billy Packer found themselves passing time during a Maryland game at Cole Field House. Packer was scouting the Terps, Driesell their opponent. The Davidson coach carried as much disdain for Maryland as the Demon Deacon assistant had had for Driesell at their first encounter years earlier. Wake Forest had been an established program and Davidson a long-running joke in 1960, when Driesell landed in Charlotte and tried to turn the Wildcats around. Driesell suffered through Davidson's 13th straight losing season in 1960–61, but his college coaching debut began with a shock, a 65-59 victory over Wake Forest that warned of a new player on Tobacco Road.

"We looked down on him because of who he was and where we were in the scheme of things," Packer said of his playing perspective, "but by now things had been reversed. He was an established head coach, and I was a young assistant, below his level. I was there to scout Maryland, and Lefty was there to scout the opponent, I think it was GW [George Washington]. There weren't 350 people in the place. We were sitting next to each other talking, and I said, 'Of all the places in the country to coach, this would have to be one of the best.' The recruiting environment, Cole Field House, the location being so close to the northern corridor. Lefty screwed his head around as if I was crazy and said, 'They don't pay nothing, here, Packer.'"

Maryland was viewed as a tired loser, and Driesell knew nothing but winning—and selling.

Charles Grice Driesell had been born on Christmas Day in 1931, the son of a jeweler. Before he was 10, Driesell earned his first varsity letter at Granby High School in Norfolk, Virginia, where he managed the football, basketball, and baseball teams until he was old enough to play for them. He played all three sports for Granby, and as a senior in 1949–50 starred on a state championship basketball team. Driesell turned down an offer from the University of Tennessee and went to Duke University, where he was a reserve for coach Harold Bradley. Media guides of the day list "Charlie" Driesell as a senior in 1953–54, the season the Atlantic

Coast Conference opened for business. Duke won the first ACC regular-season championship as Driesell averaged 5.0 points and 2.1 rebounds, and hit a shot that beat N.C. State.

Unfulfilled by a well-paying job at a Ford plant in his hometown, Driesell went back to his old school to teach and coach, and he made ends meet selling encyclopedias door to door. By 1956 he was in charge of the varsity basketball team at Granby. Three seasons at Newport News High produced a state championship and a record 57-game winning streak, and Driesell was hired by Davidson. Dwight D. Eisenhower was in the White House, and Driesell was 28.

After that initial losing season, Davidson became a force in the Southern Conference with an up-tempo game that allowed his players plenty of freedom. Driesell began a four-year run as Southern Conference Coach of the Year in 1963–64, when his Wildcats set an NCAA record for team field goal percentage. Mindful of the success that North Carolina coach Frank McGuire had achieved with New York talent, Driesell perfected the art of luring boys from the big city, but he would go anywhere for talent, and do just about anything. An early coup came in northern Virginia, where he found Fred Hetzel.

"Mrs. Hetzel had a pet snake that lived in a tree in the living room," said Joe Harrington, who assisted Driesell at Maryland. "The tree started shaking and the snake slithered onto Lefty, rolling around on his arm and leg. The mother said, 'The last coach that was in here said where he was from, they stomp snakes.' Lefty said, 'I love snakes.' Fred Hetzel was one of Lefty's first big recruits."

This familiar publicity still was Jim Kehoe's favorite. He made his mark at Maryland as an athlete, coach, and administrator, and he was the athletic director who brought Lefty Driesell to College Park in 1969. (Jim Kehoe.)

Before he starred in three sports at Norfolk's Granby High, Lefty Driesell (second row, far left) served as the school's manager. As an eighth grader in 1945, he cleaned up for a football team that won a Virginia state championship. (Buzz Sawyer.)

In 1966, Driesell lost a bitter recruiting war that would resonate through his rivalry with Dean Smith, who was clawing to make North Carolina great again. Smith had refused to schedule Davidson, which only made it more galling when slick guard Charlie Scott backed out of his commitment to Driesell and enrolled at North Carolina, which Smith hadn't gotten past the semifinals of the ACC tournament in his first five seasons. Driesell didn't come out of New York empty-handed that year, as he landed Mike Maloy, a strong, mobile big man. With Maloy starring as a sophomore in 1967–68, Driesell took little Davidson, which in the 21st century remains one of the smallest colleges playing Division I basketball, to the Eastern regional final of the NCAA tournament. The Wildcats were eliminated at Reynolds Coliseum, one win shy of the Final Four, by none other than North Carolina and Scott.

Maryland, meanwhile, had completed its first year under Frank Fellows, the top assistant who had been elevated to replace Millikan. The arrival on varsity of Hetzel's brother Will and fellow sophomore Rod Horst was about the only good news in College Park, as Billy Jones and Dick Drescher ended their Terp careers in 1968 with a dismal 8-16 record. As athletic director Bill Cobey planned for retirement, Jim Kehoe, the take-no-prisoners leader of the track and field team, was made the athletic director designate.

Kehoe's flattop and military demeanor had been familiar to two generations of Maryland students. Since 1946, he had run the intramural program, directed men's housing, and overseen one of the premier track programs in the East. Kehoe was a state product who had shown great promise as a half-miler at Bel Air High, from which he had graduated in 1936. He had starred at the Penn Relays in 1940, when the Terps won three Championship of America titles. At the Princeton Invitational he had covered 880 yards in 1 minute, 50.8 seconds, which stood as the Maryland record for 23 years. His Amateur Athletic Union title meant that Kehoe was the national champion, and he would have been in the hunt for an Olympic medal if global conflict hadn't canceled the Games.

Kehoe had served 18 months in the South Pacific, earned a Bronze Star, and been a lieutenant colonel when he retired from the U.S. Army. His track and field teams had been the class act of the ACC, as they won all but one conference title between 1954 and 1969. He ran a sharp outfit, had no stomach for incompetence or slackers, and could not for the life of him understand why Maryland football and basketball were so bad. Kehoe had built an imposing track and field program. The Maryland lacrosse team had earned a share of the national championship in 1967. The soccer team was riding the crest of a wave that would earn the Terps a share of the NCAA title in 1968. Why, Kehoe said to no one in particular and anyone who would listen, can't we be just as good in basketball and football?

Dr. Wilson Homer Elkins had nothing against big-time athletics, having earned eight varsity letters in football, basketball, and track and field at the University of Texas. After he had succeeded Curley Byrd as president of the University of Maryland in 1954, however, the focus of his stewardship had become making Maryland as renowned for its academic departments as it had been for Jim Tatum's football team. Athletic scholarships were maintained, but not at the expense of grants to stronger students. Admissions standards were raised for athletes, and graduation rates were deemed as important as winning percentages.

Maryland settled into a long period of mediocrity in the two major sports. If the Terps won, fine. If they didn't, that was all right, too. Into that lull stepped Kehoe, who immediately found himself in the middle of a major crisis that distracted him from his search for a new basketball coach. Maryland football had been a mess for much of the 1960s. Navy cited an obscene gesture by a Terp player and ended the rivalry between the state's only major college teams in 1965. Maryland is probably fortunate that it didn't schedule historically black institutions Maryland State, which later dropped football and became Maryland Eastern Shore, and Morgan State.

The hiring of Jerry Claiborne in 1972 began a turnaround, but not before the losing had continued under Roy Lester, who had been brought in by Kehoe in 1969. Granted, Kehoe was working under the duress of a player revolt that led him to fire Bob Ward, who decades earlier had been hailed as the greatest player, pound for pound, ever to toughen Maryland football. The players said they couldn't relate to Ward, whose two seasons had delivered two wins. They didn't perform for Lester either. Hired on the basis of a glittering decade at Richard Montgomery High that had produced an 86-10-1 record, Lester went 7-25 in three seasons with the Terps.

Some of the ugliness of the transition from Ward to Lester was lost amid the excitement generated by the coming of Driesell. Ward resigned on March 5, 1969. Ten days later, Driesell worked his last game for Davidson. Within 24 hours, Driesell agreed to become Maryland's coach, but it wasn't a whirlwind romance. Kehoe had been courting him all winter. In 1968–69, Fellows's second and last season as head coach, college basketball was turning a corner. The Lew Alcindor era ended at UCLA with a third straight NCAA title and LSU's Pete Maravich set a scoring record with an average of 44.2 points, Maryland won just two ACC games and attendance dipped to its lowest in five years. Fellows's vote of confidence consisted of Kehoe's proclaiming that he was the Terps' coach—until the season ended.

The previous winter, while coaching at an indoor track meet at Madison Square Garden, Kehoe had noted the excitement that Driesell had brought to Davidson. Starring for Maryland was Fred Hetzel's brother, Will, who happened to be a second-generation Terp. Kehoe had trusted booster Jack Heise contact Fred Hetzel Sr., a Maryland player from 1927 to 1930, to arrange an introduction with Driesell. Heise hit Charlotte during a blizzard, but Driesell was warmed by the thought of the camp money he could make at Maryland.

Driesell was again contending for the Final Four, and the NCAA tournament sent him to College Park for another fateful Eastern Regional. With Maloy making all 13 of his free throws, Davidson beat St. John's in one Sweet 16 game at Cole. In the other, North Carolina squeaked by Duquesne. Two days later, with 1:05 left in a tie game, the Tar Heels drew an offensive charge. They ran down the clock and Scott hit a game-winning 20-footer with three seconds left, his 10th field goal in 14 second-half shots.

Foiled for the second straight season by North Carolina and Scott, the recruit that had gotten away, Driesell stayed in College Park and faced a full-court press at Kehoe's home. The athletic director designate had told DeMatha coach and Maryland grad Morgan Wooten that if Driesell didn't agree to a contract offer within 24 hours, the job was his. As much as he liked Lester and Wooten, Kehoe did not want two high school coaches in

Under Lefty Driesell (third from left), Maryland basketball's popularity spread from the little man to power brokers. After the 1972 NIT championship, he shared a moment with (left to right) Dr. Wilson H. Elkins, the university's president; state comptroller Louis L. Goldstein; and Governor Marvin Mandel. (Maryland Sports Information.)

charge of Maryland's major sports rebirth, and Driesell clearly was his choice. The Terps could give Driesell the resources necessary to take down North Carolina and the other ACC powers that had shunned him in the past. He could pocket more summer camp revenue at Cole. He could complete Washington's coaching trinity. In the summer, there would be applause for Senators manager Ted Williams, who had been baseball's most scientific hitter. In the fall, folks would chant for Vince Lombardi, who was going to make the Redskins championship material for the first time since Sammy Baugh. Finally, in the winter, basketball fans could say amen to Driesell.

After several hours of late-night haggling, Kehoe said, Joyce Driesell told her husband to "cut" the deal, and Maryland had its man.

Four days after his season ended at Cole one victory shy of the Final Four, Driesell was introduced as the Terp coach. Davidson assistant Terry Holland agreed to follow him north, but Driesell was accompanied at the news conference by his new assistant George Raveling, who, in addition to dabbling in the sneaker business with Converse, had played and been an assistant coach at Villanova. As Driesell laid out his grand design for Maryland basketball, he remembered the breakfast conversation he'd had with Heise, Harrington, and Jay McMillen, who was hanging around College Park, hoping to get into the university's dental school in Baltimore.

"We were talking about how Maryland would be a great place for Lefty," McMillen said. "It would be uphill, but it could be like the UCLA of the East. It came out, just like that. It was unintentional, but it had a hook, like a pop song."

Driesell used the line at his news conference, and anything seemed possible, since man would walk on the moon in four months. The boast clung to him through 17 seasons and never a dull moment at Maryland. Driesell came to College Park when basketball, campus life, and society at large were undergoing great change. Winding down were the careers of old-school coaches like Henry Iba, Adolph Rupp, and John Wooden, men who let their accomplishments do the talking. It wasn't polite to brag, but they were retiring and a new generation was coming up, one that understood the possibilities of TV. Today's game is spiced by slick computer graphics and hip-hop jargon being tossed around by commentators in their 60s who should know better, but college basketball at the start of the 21st century is a bland enterprise when weighed against the product that provided such outrageous charm three decades ago.

Whether the causes are obvious, such as wall-to-wall coverage on cable networks and Internet chat rooms, or subtle, such as the movement toward political correctness in speech, coaches guard what they say, what they wear, and how they act. Men who trained to be high school physical education teachers sport designer suits and make cookie-cutter pronouncements, and it makes one long for the early 1970s. There wasn't saturation coverage, but coaches, clothing styles, and the game itself turned up the volume.

Conformity was a dirty word on campuses during the height of the Vietnam War, and a lot of coaches listened to their own drummers. As African American players followed the lead of guitarist Jimi Hendrix and sprouted Afro hairstyles, white players like Will Hetzel grew their hair, too, and confused conservatives. Coaches were supposed to represent the establishment, so how could Marquette's Al McGuire ride a motorcycle and design uniform shirts that weren't supposed to be tucked in? Team uniforms weren't nearly as garish as the get-ups of the coaches, who would wear rainbow-colored leisure suits, and then platform shoes as disco music came into favor.

The college game sprouted characters, and none was as confounding as Lefty Driesell, a paradox whose impulses could get the best of him. Forgotten players accused Driesell of abandoning them. Co-workers praised him as a family man, and the NCAA made him the first college coach to receive its Award of Valor for his role in the 1973 rescue of children and adults from a burning townhouse in Bethany Beach, Delaware.

After the biggest loss of his career, Driesell went on the opponent's bus and wished N.C. State well, but a decade later he grabbed his neck and made the choke sign at another foe. He has advanced degrees, and a devil of a time pronouncing "statistics." Driesell bathed in the affection of an appreciative crowd, but Kehoe said that "if 14,999 people left Cole happy and one wrote a letter of complaint," his coach would fire off a nasty letter right back.

Driesell is in the fifth decade of a love-hate relationship with the media, with the typical scenario that of the coach's picking a fight and asking questions later. When author John Feinstein came on the Maryland beat for the *Washington Post* in 1978, Driesell complained about a negative article that had been written nearly a decade earlier by "yo' buddy Denklinger." At Driesell's invitation, Feinstein sifted through a file marked "negative publicity." The article in question had been written not by Ken Denlinger of the *Post*, but by Steve Hershey of the *Washington Star*.

"When you write something critical, you're obliged to show up and let the coach have at you," Denlinger said. "I showed up for Lefty's press conference after a critical article, and he invited me out onto the parking lot to fight. He said, 'I've got more class in my little finger than you've got in your entire body.' It died down, and the one thing I'll always admire about Lefty is that he does those things, and then he forgets about them. A couple of weeks after he wanted to punch me out, he gave me a great anecdote for a story."

Starting with the "UCLA of the East" promise, Driesell elevated putting his foot in his mouth to an art form. For decades, critics harped over his strategy, but there was one area where his calculating was admirable. "I can coach," was the theme of many Driesell monologues, but he rarely had to say, "I can recruit."

7

FROM THE CONTROVERSIAL PURCHASE of newspaper advertising space in 1969, to taking an airplane ride with one of the top recruits in the high school Class of 1985, to not taking no for an answer in one of his final recruiting efforts at Maryland, few college coaches were as innovative and driven as Driesell when it came to getting talent. Toward the end of his tenure with the Terps, the NCAA had sharply regulated the evaluation of players and the wooing of them, but it couldn't outlaw all of Driesell's gimmicks.

Determined to keep DeMatha's Danny Ferry, a prep All-American in 1984–85, out of a Duke uniform, Driesell and assistant coach Ron Bradley picked him up in a limousine and headed to the College Park airport. When they passed over Cole, Driesell pointed out the window. Cole's curved roof was draped with a white banner, and the 40-foot black letters read "DANNY'S HOUSE." A year later, when every other college that had lost J. R. Reid to North Carolina thanked him for the privilege of having been considered by him, Driesell kept asking if he was really sure he wanted to play for the Tar Heels.

In the mid-1970s the persistence of recruiters like Driesell led the NCAA to limit a college coaching staff to three visits to a prospect's home. The NCAA manual has become a tome, with specific limits on where, when, and how often a coach can meet with a "prospective student athlete." There are restrictions on when national letters of intent can be signed and who can be included in that photo opportunity. It all saddens Driesell, who came of age when recruiting was like riding through the Wild West. There was little law on that 1960s frontier.

Gary Williams watched Terence Morris, a shy freshman forward from Frederick, squirm through a few local-boy-about-to-make-good newspaper articles in 1997 and declared him off limits to the media until the end of his first semester. When Christmas came, that embargo was pushed back to the start of the second semester. Two decades earlier, Driesell had put together a recruiting class that included Ernie Graham, Albert King, and Greg Manning, and he had had the high schoolers report to College Park to be introduced at a news conference.

Driesell successfully crashed the last Final Four played on a college campus. It was his gym, wasn't it? In 1970, the NCAA tournament culminated at Cole Field House. While graduate assistant football coach Ralph Friedgen cut a class to observe John Wooden putting UCLA through its paces on the day between the Bruins' victories over New Mexico State and Jacksonville, Driesell invited the national basketball media to a ceremony in the lobby of Cole.

Sports Illustrated noted, in its coverage of the Final Four on March 30, 1970: "Last Friday was a day of rest and rumor: Artis Gilmore earned $75 a day as a Jacksonville playground instructor last summer [true]; UCLA is going to get that tall white kid out of San Diego, Bill Walton [probably true]. It was also a day for Coach Lefty Driesell of the host University of Maryland [whose ambition it is to make his school 'the UCLA of the East'] to announce the signing of two New York City high-school stars. Lefty's press conference upstaged the team workouts at Cole Field House."

The New Yorkers were high school teammates Len Elmore and Jap Trimble, who would be in the first Maryland recruiting class that Driesell had a full year to work on, and the one that remains his most fabled.

At that 1970 Final Four, envious Maryland fans watched as Sidney Wicks, a ferocious forward for UCLA, contained Gilmore, the 7-foot-2 big man from Jacksonville. The Terps didn't have anyone with comparable talent, as any knowledgeable student on campus could tell Driesell. Dick Jerardi, a journalism major in 1969 who would go on to cover college basketball and horse racing for the *Philadelphia Daily News,* did just that when Driesell landed on campus.

"When Lefty came," Jerardi said, "me and a friend, Cesar Alsop, walked into his office and told him, 'Your team stinks, and we're your saviors.' Some of his players weren't that good. He had an open tryout, and a couple of hundred people came out. Lefty immediately cut everyone who couldn't make a layup. I did make that first cut, but he didn't keep anyone from that tryout."

It took a few seasons before the recruiting stunts toned down. Driesell invited two players from the women's team to try out for his 1973–74 powerhouse, but by then he had raised the bar and eliminated marginal prospects from Maryland's shopping list. When Driesell got the job, high school seniors who had committed to play for the Terps were told that the program no longer had scholarships for them. Lost in that shuffle was a senior at Great Mills High in St. Mary's County, a recruit who had been befriended by Billy Jones and Joe Harrington. When Tubby Smith coached Kentucky to the NCAA title in 1998, he was still peeved that he hadn't gotten a chance to play for his state university.

"LEFTY'S" NBA PLAYERS

"LEFTY'S" NBA PLAYERS

LEN ELMORE
Indiana Pacers
1st Round

TOM McMILLEN
Buffalo Braves
New York Knicks
Atlanta Hawks
1st Round

JOHN LUCAS
Houston Rockets
1st Player Picked in 1976 NBA Draft

BRAD DAVIS
Los Angeles Lakers
1st Round

MAURICE "MO" HOWARD
Cleveland Cavaliers
New Orleans Jazz
2nd Round

STEVE SHEPPARD
Chicago Bulls
2nd Round

MOSES MALONE
Houston Rockets
1st Round

DICK SNYDER
(Davidson)
Cleveland Cavaliers
1st Round

OTHER DRIESELL PLAYERS DRAFTED INTO THE NBA

Darrell Brown	Don Davidson	Jim O'Brien
Owen Brown	Fred Hetzel	Tom Roy
Bob Bodell	Jerry Kroll	Howard White
Doug Cook	Mike Malloy	Barry Yates

Driesell was after bigger fish, and the tales behind his expeditions got taller with time.

His spiel started with introductions at a high school or summer camp. Driesell was expert at determining whether a player's mother or father had greater influence on a son. Home visits were ritualized. Driesell would enter, followed by an assistant bearing a briefcase. After his sales pitch on academics and the benefits of playing near the nation's capital, Driesell would ask for the briefcase, which contained a Maryland jersey with the prospect's name on the back. He knew how to make himself at home. In 1972, Mo Howard was the top prospect in Philadelphia's Catholic league. A voracious eater, Driesell once walked into Howard's house, went straight to the kitchen, and sampled some strawberry short-cake before dinner.

On campus visits in the 1970s, recruits could be introduced to the crowd, which was expected to make the student feel welcome. Howard

Moses Malone (lower right) never attended a Maryland class or practiced with the Terps, but Lefty Driesell didn't mind including him in the 1977–78 media guide among his players who had gone on to play professionally. (Jim Kehoe.)

got that treatment, and still gets gooseflesh thinking of it. As No. 8 North Carolina whipped Maryland, 100-76, on February 17, 1971, Tom Roy, the best big man in New England, experienced the red-carpet treatment and its accompanying turf wars.

"I had the ability to go anywhere," Roy said. "Carolina was one of the schools after me, and they were annihilating Maryland. I was sitting near the tunnel entrance, and as the players were leaving the floor, their little guard said, 'That's why you want to go to North Carolina.' It was George Karl. Lefty got a little bit perturbed by that."

One of Driesell's last great recruiting catches was Albert King, who was a man-child in the summer of 1974, when Rick Telander followed the New York pickup basketball scene and made the 14-year-old one of the two key figures in his book *Heaven Is a Playground*. As he prepared to enter the 10th grade, King embarrassed older men on the playgrounds at night, worked in an agent's office during the day, and considered the hard sell of a prep school in Pennsylvania that wanted him badly. The cards and letters from college coaches, including Driesell, were already coming.

That was a bittersweet summer for Driesell. At the Dapper Dan Classic in Pittsburgh, the cutting-edge all-star game that was run by Sonny Vaccaro, Maryland had the inside track on both MVPs, Brad Davis for the locals and Moses Malone for the national team. The Terps won the battle for Malone but lost the war, as the center from Petersburg, Virginia, signed a letter of intent to attend Maryland and then a professional contract with the Utah Stars of the American Basketball Association before he enrolled. Two years before the NBA accepted early-entry candidates, Malone's move was revolutionary.

Malone's recruitment was as bizarre as they come. An assistant from New Mexico lived full time in Petersburg in order to keep tabs on the best post prospect since Alcindor. An introvert who didn't like the attention, Malone would hide under his bed to duck recruiters. He was lying on it when he signed a letter of intent with Maryland. Malone's high school coach said that the Terps won his signature because they got to him first and never let up in their attention. That included visits from Dave Pritchett, a recent hire from Boston College who was better known as "Pit Stop" for his need to maintain hands-on contact with prospects.

Pit Stop drank coffee by the pot, not the cup. In the morning, he would wake up and drive to Baltimore so he could bump into Larry Gibson at Dunbar High. There would be a quick flight to Pittsburgh, then a drive to Monaca High to see Davis. Then on to Cleveland to keep in touch with Lawrence Boston. By nightfall, Pritchett could make Buffalo, or maybe Memphis. Newspaper accounts have exaggerated it to eight, but Pritchett cannot recall if his personal record for rental cars leased in one day was five or six. He loathed expense accounts, and his inability to hold on to receipts led to a running battle with athletic director Jim Kehoe, who argued that Pritchett spent more on recruiting travel than the entire football staff.

Organization was not Pit Stop's strong suit. After his playing days at Maryland were done, Billy Hahn got into coaching and was invited to join Pritchett's staff at Davidson in 1976. Hahn cut short his honeymoon and checked into the first assistant's office. It was occupied. So was the second assistant's office. Hahn knew something was amiss when he couldn't locate an office for a third assistant. But who needs a desk when you've got a college-issued Ford LTD? Hahn logged 98,000 miles in one year scouting talent for Pritchett.

A native of a coal-mining town in West Virginia, Pritchett climbed the coaching ranks from Bluefield State College to Virginia Commonwealth to BC. Along the way he befriended Howard Garfinkel, the founder of the Five-Star camps, who gave Pritchett a heads up about prospects and a place to crash in Queens during his hundreds of scouting missions through New York. Pritchett was a regular at a camp in the Pocono Mountains that was run by Dave Bing, the Hall of Fame guard who was then at the height of his powers with the Detroit Pistons. There Malone put on a show and beat the seasoned NBA veteran in a game of one-on-one, in front of campers and college coaches.

"Moses blocked all of David's shots, and beat him in front of a crowd of people," Pritchett said. "Bing was mad, made the kid come back, and physically beat him up, but word spread about what Malone was capable of."

Howard White saw Driesell and Maryland recruit from both sides. As an assistant coach, White spent much of 1974 in Petersburg, working his Virginia ties to Malone. Seven years earlier, when White was entering his junior year at Kecoughtan High in Hampton, Driesell had come to town to sell Davidson. When Driesell went to Maryland and added George Raveling to his staff, the product changed but the pitch remained the same.

"The first time I met him, Lefty came through town in a red Cadillac," White said. "I was looking at Davidson, North Carolina, Kansas, and Virginia, but then Maryland became one of those schools. Lefty and Raveling, they're recruiters now. They talked about winning championships, taking over the city of Washington, D.C., and the Atlantic Coast Conference, taking over all of college basketball. I did believe them."

With the program slapping together its first recruiting class, a Raveling brainstorm led to the purchase of advertising space in the

Washington Post. The M Club was supposed to pay the bill, but at the 11th hour booster Jack Heise wrote out the check for the newspaper ad that targeted four local players. Jim O'Brien from Falls Church, Virginia, was already on board, but the Terps made a very public appeal to keep DeMatha's James Brown from attending Harvard.

"Driesell gave me a heads up that he was getting ready to run the ad," O'Brien said. "It was probably the last time he ever asked me what I thought."

Kehoe said that he was kept in the dark over running the ad, which drew the scrutiny of the NCAA and a warning not to do it again. "We had to have a hearing with the NCAA," Kehoe said. "Lefty's office was next to mine, and it was a revolving door. Lefty or one of his assistants would ask, 'Can we do this, can we do that?' We did not have compliance officers or people researching the NCAA rule book to ensure that we dotted an I or crossed a T."

The class that included O'Brien, White, Pittsburgh's Darrell Brown, and Bob Bodell of Frankfort, Kentucky, was just a dry run for the effort that landed a remarkable group the following year. In 1991, Michigan would have its Fab Five, a freshman class that included Chris Webber, Juwan Howard, and Jalen Rose. In 1997, Duke would bring in a landmark class that featured William Avery, Shane Battier, and Elton Brand. The Terps had that kind of crop in 1970.

Elmore and Trimble, an athletic guard, were teammates from Power Memorial. The long of it was Mark Cartwright, a 7-footer from Morton Grove, Illinois; the short of it was Rich Porac, a guard from Monroeville, Pennsylvania. What was a fine class became distinctive at the 11th hour, when Driesell got revenge on North Carolina coach Dean Smith for winning away Charlie Scott, the New York guard who had shifted his

Lefty Driesell was involved in some intense recruiting battles, none longer than the one that landed Tom McMillen. While still a freshman at Maryland, McMillen earned recognition from President Richard M. Nixon, which he thinks affected his grade-point average. (Hornbake Library.)

commitment from Davidson to the Tar Heels in 1966, which probably knocked Driesell out of a couple of Final Fours.

Driesell's first staff included Raveling and Terry Holland, who quickly returned to Davidson after the peripatetic Larry Brown changed his mind about taking the Wildcat job. To replace Holland, Driesell brought in Jim Maloney, who had been fired by Niagara, where he had had a flashy guard named Calvin Murphy and a losing record. Driesell had no interest in retaining anyone from the former staff until he saw Joe Harrington's ties to the McMillen family. Harrington had been a close friend and teammate of Jay McMillen, who had left Maryland as its No. 2 all-time scorer in 1967. His younger brother Tom was 6-11, a big left-hander who possessed a better shooting range. McMillen was splashed on the cover of *Sports Illustrated* as the nation's best high school player, even though he played for Mansfield High in a remote region of Pennsylvania and Walton was playing in San Diego.

"Coach Driesell wasn't going to hire me, because he didn't want anything to do with anyone left over from the previous staff," Harrington said of 1969. "He wanted to clean house. That spring, we got in the car and drove up to Hershey for the Pennsylvania state tournament to watch Tom play. We walked in the hotel and I said, 'Hey, Mrs. McMillen!' She walked by Coach Driesell and gave me a hug and a kiss. From then on, there was no way I wasn't going to be on the staff. I had roomed with Jay for four years, at Bel Air Hall. One summer, I think it was 1966, I lived with Jay in Mansfield. We coached Tom's Little League baseball team. We played basketball in the backyard every night, and Jay and I would beat the crap out of Tom. His dad would sit on the porch and smoke a cigar, and tell Tom to toughen up."

Tom McMillen grew up sorting through all the recruiting sales pitches. Although a desire to remain a reasonable driving distance from his parents ruled out the West Coast, he still went to Los Angeles to visit UCLA and USC. Virginia knew of his interest in medicine and arranged for McMillen to witness an operation. When he was at West Virginia, Mountaineer coach Bucky Waters took him to a reception to meet President Lyndon B. Johnson. Maryland had the political angle covered, however, as U.S. Senator Joe Tydings took him to lunch in the Senate dining room.

McMillen waffled through the first eight months of 1970. He made a commitment to North Carolina in June, but his parents wouldn't bless it, and family matters ruled what at the time had been the most controversial recruitment of a high school basketball player. McMillen's brother Paul was a banker in Chapel Hill, and the NCAA wanted to know if that position was an improper inducement on Dean Smith's part. His other brother, of course, had been Maryland's best player in the 1960s. Jay, the first half of the duo that would become the highest-scoring tandem of brothers in ACC history, had trouble coming to grips with unsolicited appeals to get him into the University of Maryland medical school.

"In April of 1970, right after Tom finished his high school season, I received verbal notice that I had been accepted into medical school," Jay said. "In July, I was put on the waiting list. I didn't say anything to my family, and dropped out of dental school. In September, when he [Tom] decided to go to Maryland, my family thinks I'm at med school. Everyone thinks there's this quid pro quo, that I got into med school and then Tom comes, but a month later, I was twiddling my thumbs when I got a call. Three people had dropped out. It was four days before the first anatomy test. I said, 'Screw it, I'm coming.' I took the exam and got a B, half the class failed, and I realized it was not quite what it seemed, that I wasn't a dumb jock after all. I did extra work and got to know my professors, who told me that every time somebody put in a good word for me in admissions, it was a black mark against me. One of the myths that I had to live with was that Tom's coming may have moved me up on the waiting list."

In August 1970, Tom toured Europe and the Soviet Union with an Olympic development team that included Julius Erving and Dennis Wuycik, a North Carolina forward who pushed the Tar Heels. As Labor Day came and went, McMillen still hadn't made up his mind, which was swayed by his father's failing health. When September 10 and the deadline for registration dawned, Dean Smith was in Switzerland honoring a clinic commitment. Virginia coach Bill Gibson eventually had to leave the McMillen home, and Jay had his car gassed up and ready to take Tom to College Park. McMillen enrolled at Maryland at the last possible moment, spurring Smith for Driesell and leading to second-guessing that he continues more than three decades later.

"I had packed for school, even though I didn't know where I was going," McMillen said. "Bill Gibson flew up to my hometown, where he had coached for 15 years, ready to take me to Virginia. When I went to bed, he was playing bridge with my parents. In the morning, he and my parents were still playing cards. We had called my brother Jay and told him to get up here. Bill Gibson thought he was going to put me on the plane, but there came a point when he had to go back to Charlottesville. Dean had fallen out of favor with my parents a little bit. He was in Europe, and that was Dean's mistake. I probably would have gone to Carolina if Dean hadn't gone to Europe. I would have stuck to my guns."

8

ATHLETIC DIRECTOR JIM KEHOE cited four hires that turned College Park into an enchanting destination for football and basketball players.

Driesell attracted some of the East's top basketball recruits. Jerry Claiborne's arrival in 1972 began a revival in football that would net six Atlantic Coast Conference championships between 1974 and 1985. Colonel Tom Fields, a trusted track and field teammate of Kehoe's who had compiled quite a record as a Marine, having served at Guadalcanal, Korea, and Vietnam over three decades, became the executive director of the Maryland Educational Foundation. That fancy title meant that he was in charge of expanding fund-raising and the ranks of the Terrapin Club. The other piece of the puzzle was Russ Potts, who returned to campus in 1970 and made sure that the region—nay, the nation—paid attention to the transformation that Maryland basketball was undergoing. Potts had graduated from Maryland in 1964 with a degree in journalism. When he wasn't organizing events at the Phi Delta Theta fraternity, he worked for the *Diamondback* and railed against Bud Millikan.

"I never went to a Maryland game that had more than 10,000 people when I was a student," Potts said. "I lambasted him [Millikan]. I thought he deserved it. He was a tremendous Xs and Os coach, but he was a horrible recruiter. I thought there was no reason Maryland shouldn't be competitive."

Eventually given the title of assistant athletic director for advertising and promotions, Potts helped Driesell turn Maryland basketball into an event. Kehoe said that Potts "could sell an Eskimo an icebox," but acknowledged that his promoter could be "overly exuberant."

"We were the first college in the country to have a sports marketing director," Potts said. "We went from an old, dilapidated scoreboard at Cole to installing the first in the nation with commercial advertising. We went from one radio station to 55; now it's down to seven. I knew we had to get on WBAL in Baltimore, and I went to Al Burke, the general manager, 11 times before he said yes. I know that was the number because WBAL used to call itself 'Radio 11.' He finally said, 'If you promise never to bother me again, I'll take your games.' We developed a regional television package."

There is nothing reserved about Potts, a Virginia state senator who is still involved in the promotion of college basketball games. He had the pull and cash guarantees to end a lengthy feud between Driesell and John Thompson and bring them together in a 1990 double-header that pitted the latter's Georgetown against Providence and the former's James Madison against South Alabama. Potts had turned Southern Methodist University football into a happening in the late 1970s, when the Cowboys were the only game in Dallas. He quotes 19th-century showman P. T. Barnum, and there was no limit to the lengths to which Potts would go to promote Maryland basketball and Driesell, a willing subject.

The genesis of "Midnight Madness," the custom of starting practice as midnight becomes October 15, can be traced to Driesell and Maryland. A track circled the field at Byrd Stadium in 1971, and Driesell had his players report there for a timed distance run, which commenced at 12:03 A.M. On the day that the NCAA allowed formal practices to begin, Driesell had adopted the custom of scheduling dawn workouts, and he said that he had pushed it up to midnight to get a jump on the competition. Sports information director Jack Zane invited the media to that run, however, and the players understood that it wasn't going to make them a better team.

"It was a publicity stunt," said Billy Hahn, a freshman that season. "Lefty was unbelievable at getting attention."

Three decades later, Driesell's schtick and Potts's sales tactics still seem over the top. There was the boast that Maryland would be "the UCLA of the East." Moses Malone never sat in a Maryland classroom or wore a Terp uniform, but media guides in the late 1970s included him among Driesell's players in the NBA. Driesell's entrance on court was accompanied by "Hail to the Chief," a tune supposedly reserved for the arrival of the President of the United States. Some academics complained that playing it for Driesell was in bad taste, but Potts said politicians loved it. Potts introduced themed promotions, and later recalled that an uncooperative elephant had delayed the second half of the game on Circus Night.

"The elephant was stubborn, and we couldn't get him out of the tunnel," Potts said. "I thought Kehoe was going to kill me. I told him, 'You talk to the elephant, he won't listen to me.' We only did that Circus Night that once."

Even when there wasn't a game at Maryland, there was still a show. Driesell made the remarks at the first team awards banquet, which soon took on some serious star power. Track and field legend Jesse Owens, the star of the 1936 Olympics, stopped by in 1971, followed by Red

Auerbach, the architect of the Boston Celtics dynasty. Then came Kentucky coaching legend Adolph Rupp and Bill Russell, the Celtics center who had defined winning. John Wooden was the guest speaker in 1975, a few weeks after he had won the last of his ten NCAA titles and retired as the coach at UCLA. Al McGuire came by in 1977, after he had guided Marquette to the NCAA championship and gotten out of coaching.

All of those charismatic men seemed mundane in 1976, when the nation's Bicentennial year brought a visitor who transcended sport.

Potts had reserved a large ballroom at the Sheraton Lanham for that year's team banquet, but was pressured to move. A prizefight was to be held at the nearby Capital Centre and one of the boxers in need of a place to spar wanted to build a makeshift gym in the hotel's ballroom. Driesell and Potts relented under one condition: that the fighter attend the Maryland team banquet.

That's how John Lucas and Mo Howard got to meet The Greatest, Muhammad Ali.

Millikan and Frank Fellows coached in a visitor-friendly environment, as the closest fans could get to the floor for regular-season games at Cole in the 1950s and 1960s was in the 12,230 permanent seats, no closer than 30 feet to the sidelines. One afternoon, Potts, Driesell, and some of his players were among the work crew that set up risers and folding chairs on the floor, and the experiment was permanently endorsed by the administration. Like the Boy Scouts, the men behind the Maryland basketball program were being prepared, because attendance in Driesell's first season averaged below 10,000.

Attendance would soon rise.

With Jim O'Brien and Howard White on the freshman team and Driesell biding his time with Will Hetzel and other holdovers, Maryland went 13-13 in 1969–70. The Terps were 5-9 in the ACC, a sixth-place finish with talent more suited to the cellar. The high-water mark came in a two-point win over Duke on January 28, which led the pep band to put its brass to the spiritual "Amen."

The Terps' promotion and promise came together during Driesell's second season, when Maryland was still a curio item, full of flare and braggadocio, but in need of some on-court success to be taken seriously as a basketball school. More failure had come on December 16, 1970, when the Terps took a 4-0 team to South Carolina and literally got beat up. When Maryland departed for Columbia, McMillen was tearing it up on the freshman team and fellow rookie Elmore was nursing a knee injury. Of more immediate concern to Driesell, Jim O'Brien couldn't make the trip south, as he was hospitalized with internal bleeding that was diagnosed as an ulcer.

After South Carolina threatened to back out of its 1971 trip to Cole, Maryland administrators pleaded for calm, and the Maryland Medieval Mercenary Militia did their part to protect the Gamecocks. (Hornbake Library.)

Without the sophomore who would lead the Terps' scoring in 1970–71, the Terps took a big tumble against the nation's No. 2 team. White had 38 points and was endangering the gym scoring record—Maryland contended that South Carolina would not allow a black player that distinction—when John Ribock and Terp junior Charlie Blank tangled, going for a rebound. Maryland's Jay Flowers locked up with Rick Aydlett, and the scuffles quickly escalated into a brawl. Driesell said he was punched by Ribock, as officials suspended the game with 4:52 left and South Carolina cruising, 96-70.

Arguments over who had struck whom spiraled as Zane fought past security and into the Terp locker room, where he says he found Driesell in full bunker mentality.

"You gonna talk to the media?" Zane said.

"No," Lefty snapped.

"That will make South Carolina happy," Zane said.

"What do you mean?" Lefty huffed.

"They closed your locker room. South Carolina says you can't talk to the media," Zane answered.

"They're not telling me who I can't talk to," said Driesell, who reversed his own policy and opened his locker room to the media. He was still ready to fight Ribock.

"I'm going to get me a lawyer and sue that SOB," Driesell told the *Baltimore Evening Sun*'s Bill Tanton, who had made a fortuitous road trip at a time when the Baltimore-Washington media weren't yet in the practice of traveling with Maryland. Driesell ripped South Carolina coach Frank McGuire for letting his team get out of control. McGuire alluded to the impetuosity of youth and said, "I'm smarter than some of these guys who get too excited." Driesell predicted "trouble at College Park" for the rematch. A day later, the president of South Carolina said he "deeply regretted" the fight in a telegram he sent to Maryland President Wilson H. Elkins, but McGuire remained unrepentant. He told reporters that Driesell "hit himself in the mouth," called for the Federal Bureau of Investigation to look into the matter, and asked that South Carolina's game at Cole be canceled.

The Gamecocks were preparing to depart the ACC, a shift that in hindsight proved disastrous for their basketball program. South Carolina was made out to be a villain in the ACC, and McGuire's big, bad New Yorkers relished being portrayed as goons. They had graduated likable guard Bobby Cremins, and Ribock, 6-8 and 240 pounds, was the smallest starter on their front line. Norvall Neve, the acting commissioner of the ACC, threatened to move the game, but Kehoe hunkered down and guaranteed protection for the Gamecocks. Two days before the rematch on January 9, 1971, he paid for a full-page ad in the *Diamondback.* Photos of Driesell and Kehoe flanked one of a packed Cole, above a plea for restraint:

TO ALL MARYLAND BASKETBALL STUDENTS AND FANS

We extend a cordial welcome to the very fine basketball team from the University of South Carolina that will be visiting us on Saturday, January 9.

In reply to those Carolina fans, and others, who have written or called expressing concern regarding the possibility of 'incidents' during this game, we have made the following statement:

The students at the University of Maryland will accord Coach McGuire and his Carolina team the same warm welcome, courteous treatment and gracious hospitality which we offer to all guests on our campus.

Coach Driesell, his staff, and the Terrapin basketball team join us in requesting that this pledge be honored. We are asking your wholehearted support.

The Athletic Department

What followed was one of the strangest nights in the history of Cole, as a game that was hyped as World War III had as much first-half action as a kindergarten shoving match. Coming off its first loss of the season, by 15 points at North Carolina, a tentative South Carolina team didn't know what to expect. After McMillen had poured in 41 points in a freshman rout of Villanova, the "Maryland Medieval Mercenary Militia," a group of students who played dress-up in the summer and might moonlight at today's Renaissance fairs, ringed the court and faced the stands as the Gamecocks warmed up. Decked out in faux chain mail and with

First-half action was limited on January 9, 1971, when South Carolina stayed in its zone against Maryland's slowdown tactics. South Carolina's Tom Riker (51), Kevin Joyce (43), and John Ribock (41) showed their disdain while the Terps' Sparky Still (24) waited for a pass from Jim O'Brien that probably didn't come. (News American collection.)

tongues firmly in cheek, they brandished mock shields and swords, prepared to defend South Carolina from the menacing Maryland horde.

Within days, hard hats became part of the attire at high school games throughout the state. "You had students on the floor, dressed like they were going to war," White said. "When South Carolina came to Cole for the rematch, it was crazy, with people hanging from the rafters."

South Carolina was introduced to silence, the crowd of 14,312 went berserk as Maryland's starters were announced, and the Gamecocks were immediately on their heels. They were thrown even more off guard when the Terps held the ball, legal since the 35-second shot clock wouldn't be adopted until 1985.

"South Carolina always played a 2-3 zone, that's all they ever did," said Joe Harrington, then an assistant coach. "We were going to play two-on-two with Howard White and Jim O'Brien, and make them come out of their zone and guard us."

Thirty years later, Driesell said, "I will do anything legal to win a basketball game." Harrington said that Driesell was an underrated tactician who had saved the scouting report of his first win at Davidson in

When South Carolina came to Cole in 1971, Maryland fans were on their best behavior until Jim O'Brien's overtime basket led to a wild celebration that Lefty Driesell likened to that of a football crowd. (Hornbake Library.)

1960. Maryland had made a dry run the previous season, when it had slowed things down at South Carolina and stayed within 11. N.C. State had done the same, and beat the Gamecocks in a double-overtime 1970 ACC tournament final that produced a combined total of 81 points. O'Brien, who had listened to the fight game on the radio and seen photos of "12,000 people at the Coliseum coming after my teammates," had a different recollection.

"I don't believe we worked on the slowdown at all," O'Brien said of Maryland's preparation. "I went by the bench one time, and he [Driesell] said, 'Let's bring them out of the zone.' We may have been planning to play a slow pace, but it turned into complete dead ball."

The home team didn't score in the first 11 minutes. Maryland held the ball for stretches that lasted 8 minutes, 35 seconds, and 7 minutes, 31 seconds, in the first half, which ended with a jumper by White that gave the Terps a 4-3 lead. A photographer for the *Washington Post* rushing his film to a courier ran past Zane and announced that he had caught every basket—all three of them. A more comfortable pace was restored in the second half, when McGuire ditched his zone, but Maryland wasn't about to run with South Carolina. There were seven ties in the second half, the last coming in the closing seconds, when O'Brien controlled a missed free throw by White and put in a reverse lay-in that forced overtime.

The Gamecocks quickly asserted themselves and had a 30-25 lead with 24 seconds left in the extra session, when, as White said, "miraculous stuff started happening." O'Brien scored, White stole John Roche's inbounds pass, and Dick Stobaugh cut the deficit to one. Bob Bodell cut in front of Kevin Joyce and picked off another inbounds pass from Roche. The ball went from White to O'Brien, who finished a perfect 6-for-6 shooting night with two seconds left and gave Maryland a monumental 31-30 victory.

Before Juan Dixon came to Maryland and put his stamp on the 2002 NCAA tournament, O'Brien's game-winner might have been the biggest basket in the program's history.

Celebrating Maryland's first conquest of a Top 10 team in six seasons, students and adults rushed out of the stands and onto the floor. Players ran for cover, and the Terrapin mascot had the presence of mind to pluck the smallest manager off the Terp bench and plop him on his shoulders. "The place was a madhouse," said Chuck Driesell, Lefty's son, who was a wide-eyed second-grader. "The turtle put me on his shoulders, so I wouldn't get crushed."

Driesell told newspapermen that it had been "one of the greatest nights of my life." South Carolina's flat-footed front line of Ribock and two 6-10 players, Tom Owens and Tom Riker, teamed for one rebound, and Maryland fans owned the boards as much as the Terps. The toppling of goalposts is a football tradition, but basket supports? Students climbed atop them, but the repair bill was worth the publicity, as Maryland got national notice for something other than Driesell's recruiting.

"The Terps' heroes were two sophomore guards, Howard White, a hot dog who showed up for a team picture with a derby and umbrella, and Jim O'Brien, a newly cool cat," *Sports Illustrated* reported in its January 18, 1971, edition. "O'Brien, it develops, has an ulcer. His doctor ordered him last week not to think about the game, 'so I thought how nice it would be to spend the evening skating on the lake near my home in Falls Church [Virginia].'"

The result was an anomaly. South Carolina got revenge in the quarterfinals of the conference tournament in Greensboro, where it beat Maryland, 71-63. The Gamecocks edged North Carolina by 1 in the championship game, then got handled by unbeaten Pennsylvania in their NCAA opener. McGuire pulled out of the ACC and took South Carolina to the next three NCAA tournaments, but the Gamecocks haven't won an NCAA game since 1973.

Did the upset generate any momentum for Maryland? After the slowdown, the Terps went 3-7 in the ACC en route to another sixth-place finish. The overall record of 14-12 was a net improvement of one game, but Driesell gauged his freshman team and rubbed his hands.

9

THE FRESHMEN WHO HAD GONE 16-0 in 1970–71 moved up to the varsity, and Maryland basketball was changed forever. Tom McMillen had appeared on the cover of the 1971–72 media guide, greeting two fans not typically associated with college basketball, President Richard Nixon and his wife, Pat. Absent from the national Top 10 since 1958, when the program had made its lone trip to the NCAA tournament, the precocious Terps began the season ranked No. 6 in the land. Maryland was ready to begin a steady run that would take it to new heights, but its timing was terrible, as the Terps ran into the best player in the history of the Atlantic Coast Conference and came out on the short end of a 1974 ACC tournament final that is regarded as the most compelling, best-played game in conference history.

The star in question, the high-flying David Thompson, had been a freshman at N.C. State during the 1971–72 season, but he had been in-eligible to play for the Wolfpack, and the most talked-about newcomer on Tobacco Road was Bob McAdoo, an elastic 6-9 combination of power, hops, and scoring savvy who was good enough to make Dean Smith lift his embargo against junior-college transfers. McAdoo elevated North Carolina, which pounded the Terps by 20 in Chapel Hill on January 29, but Maryland sent a salvo across the broadside of the ACC establishment in the rematch in College Park. On February 16, 1972, the largest crowd in the history of the ACC crammed into Cole, as 15,287 saw McMillen score 27 and Howard White put in two free throws with seven seconds left in overtime for a 79-77 conquest of the Tar Heels. The Terps, who had just one senior, reserve Charlie Blank, would notch a school-record 27 wins and roll through the National Invitation Tournament. They had been shunted to that consolation affair because, while Maryland had reached the ACC final for the first time since 1958, it had lost to North Carolina, and the NCAA still accepted only one team per conference.

That 1972 ACC tournament final had been a harbinger of things to come for Driesell, who later would experience near total frustration against Smith, as Maryland went 3-20 against North Carolina in the decade before Len Bias closed his career with a flourish against the Tar

Heels. Before that drought began in 1976, Maryland briefly held the upper hand, as it went 4-3 against North Carolina from 1973 to 1975. Unfortunately for Driesell, North Carolina wasn't the team to beat in the ACC.

Maryland thought it was. The Terps were good, and they knew it, as Driesell had put together an engaging mix that was a publicist's dream, glib young men who had something to say in one of the most tumultuous times of the 20th century. O'Brien and White were completing their freshman year in May 1970, when approximately 1,000 students protesting President Nixon's decision to send troops into Cambodia set fires on campus that did an estimated $25,000 in damage. The year McMillen left campus, the Vietnam War came to a climax and Nixon resigned in the wake of the Watergate scandal. The most requested photo in the National Archives was a 1970 publicity still of Nixon and Elvis Presley, and McMillen argues that his own photo opportunity with the president cost him.

"We had riots on campus, tear gas," McMillen said. "I was in premed, determined to get good grades. I had a 4.0 my freshman year, and one B my senior year, in speech class. This woman really got mad at me. Here I'm taking chemistry and getting As, so I couldn't understand a B in speech. I was on the cover of the *Washington Post* with Richard Nixon shaking my hand when I was appointed to the President's Council on Physical Fitness. Because Nixon was so hated with the liberal university crowd, that was held against me in that class."

A few scraped by academically, but Elmore wondered if his Maryland teams were "too cerebral." He would eventually earn a law degree at Harvard, while McMillen passed the rigorous standards for a Rhodes scholarship and studied in Oxford, England. A teammate said McMillen got the publicity, but that reserve forward Owen Brown was just as sharp. John Lucas, the freshman point guard, was the son of a high school principal. After bed check on the road, McMillen would move the lamp off the nightstand and under his covers to study a textbook, which some thought was a bit much. Elmore, who was host of a show on the campus radio station, seemed just as aloof.

"We received so many conflicting messages, with regard to life, studies, athletics," Elmore said. "When everyone on the team was housed in Cambridge Hall, I went to Ellicott. When they moved to Ellicott, I went to Hagerstown. I tried to run away from them. I knew that my teammates would laugh at all of my jokes, and I wanted to meet people beyond basketball. We were able to make choices for ourselves. Now, I worry that choices are made for players."

There had been too many Terps to satisfy, as any fan who took in one of their barnstorming intersquad games around the state could see.

In 1972 an NCAA limitation of one team per conference shunted Maryland to the National Invitation Tournament, which was ruled by a sophomore class that included center Len Elmore (41). (News American collection.)

There were enough prep All-Americans practicing in Cole to choose sides and play full court, but seven-footer Mark Cartwright, Donald White, and Varick Cutler left nearly as quickly as they arrived, and Wilson Washington's Maryland career consisted of one game.

In 1972–73, Lucas and fellow freshman Mo Howard got more playing time than returning players Rich Porac and Hahn, who still schooled them in practice sometimes. Driesell would be irked when Howard and Lucas took it easy in practice. One of the best all-white backcourts ever was starring in Los Angeles at the time, and Hahn and Porac idolized Jerry West and Gail Goodrich of the NBA's Lakers. West was bigger than the left-handed Goodrich, and Hahn was bigger than the left-handed Porac.

"Nice shot, Jerry," Porac would say after a basket by Hahn in practice.

"Nice pass, Gail," Hahn would answer.

Hahn had been schooled in the fundamentals on Indiana farmland, Elmore on New York blacktops, as Driesell gathered all sorts of talent from all sorts of backgrounds. By 1972–73, he had stockpiled jump shooters like McMillen, low-post forces like Elmore, defensive stoppers like Bob Bodell, and conductors like Lucas. In age they ranged from the veteran O'Brien to the rookie Lucas, who was handed the ball as Howard White recovered from a serious knee injury. Lucas had made *Sports Illustrated*'s "Faces in the Crowd" for his prowess in both basketball and tennis. Tom Roy said, "With Mac [McMillen] and Luke [Lucas], you needed two balls, and we only had one," but the young guard, who would go on to become a head coach in the NBA, could handle a team as well as a racket.

"Luke was a cocky son of a gun," Elmore said. "I think he used that to mask his self-doubt, but he never let that be communicated to anyone around him. The great part was the way he developed into a leader, particularly as a sophomore. Tom and myself had taken over leadership, but when it came to running the show, it was John's. It was refreshing, how much he believed in himself. He was magnetic, and people were drawn to him. He didn't relate to myself or Tom or Jim O'Brien, but he recognized that he had the ball in his hands. He had to be diplomatic, because he took the ball away from Howard White, but Luke thought he should have been playing anyway. That was his edge. He was an extension of Lefty. Sometimes he could be manipulative, but he had a brashness and a self-belief that coach loved."

While Lucas was getting acclimated to campus life in September 1972, McMillen was in Munich, Germany, playing for none other than U.S. coach Henry Iba at the Olympics. With McMillen's ailing father as his companion, Driesell took a day trip into the backwoods of Bavaria in search of his ancestral home. Tom followed in horror as Palestinian terrorists took 11 Israeli athletes hostage in the Olympic village and massacred them all. Five days later, the basketball outcome outraged Americans, as the U.S. men fell for the first time in international play. The loss to the Soviet Union was attributed to inept and corrupt officiating, but the Americans scored just 50 points in the gold-medal game, and Iba was blamed for forcing his plodding tactics on an athletic team that included Doug Collins.

Professionalism was still a dirty word at the Olympics, and the Dream Team was two decades off, but the United States still didn't have its best on-campus talent. The U.S. Olympic Committee demanded that interested players try out, but Bill Walton refused and stayed home at UCLA, following the Grateful Dead instead of Iba. N.C. State was represented by 7-foot-4 Tom Burleson, but no one argued that he was the Wolfpack's best player, not when there was a sophomore in Raleigh who was about to go on to a three-year run that remains unparalleled in the history of the ACC.

Michael Jordan, the greatest basketball player ever, was subdued by Smith's system during his three seasons at North Carolina. Ralph Sampson was an extraordinary big man, but his legacy at Virginia was tainted by a series of March mishaps. When it comes to a singular talent making an impact on the ACC and all of college basketball, Thompson was in a class of his own. All he did was become the first to be named conference Player of the Year three straight seasons and deliver the only disruption to John Wooden's UCLA dynasty between 1967 and 1975.

On a roster Thompson read like a tweener, a player too slow to play guard and too small to play forward, but his 6-foot-4 frame packed some of the best spring ever seen on a hardwood floor. Lew Alcindor led the NCAA to outlaw the dunk in 1967, and the ban wasn't lifted until 1976, a year after the game was safe from Thompson. It didn't matter; he jumped

Tom McMillen (54) brought a wide array of offensive skills to Maryland, where he compiled 1,807 points, the most ever by a Terp in the years when the NCAA didn't allow freshmen to play varsity. (Hornbake Library.)

over smaller defenders with a feathery jump shot or drove past larger ones with acrobatic moves, and he played above the rim decades before that phrase entered basketball's vocabulary.

As a freshman, Thompson was ineligible to play in 1971–72, but the Terps knew that something dangerous was looming down south. Lucas was that rarest of commodities, a personality capable of drowning out Driesell, but he knew there was someone just as good where he had come from, another country boy ready to dominate the city game.

"Luke was from Durham, and he always told us stories about this guy he used to play pick-up against," Howard said. "Donald Washington [whose career at North Carolina was cut short by an injury] was one of the five best players in the country. Luke told us that Washington went up for a shot in the corner, and David Thompson jumped up and grabbed the ball out of the air. I'm from Philadelphia. We play the boys from New York and D.C. every year, and there's no way they're playing basketball like that in North Carolina. I grew up with Big Five basketball, and I didn't know anything about the ACC. Nobody was better than Howard Porter or Kenny Durrett or Mike Bantom. Boy, was I in for a rude awakening. I was in total disbelief until I saw him with my own eyes."

Thompson's first visit to Cole was a landmark event. UCLA's dynasty played in the Pacific time zone and televised college basketball remained a rumor in many regions, so some of the Maryland brass were skeptical when it was proposed that the Terps' home game with N.C. State be televised nationally. It was the lead-in to Super Bowl VII, and January 14, 1973, wasn't a good day inside the Capital Beltway. The Redskins' offense was shut out in a 14-7 loss to the Miami Dolphins, and Thompson frustrated the Terps and their fans for the first of many times.

Off to the best start in their history, the Terps were 10-0 and ranked No. 2 when No. 3 State invaded Cole on Super Bowl Sunday. Thompson's supporting cast ranged from the 7-4 Burleson to 5-7 point guard Monte Towe, with Baltimore Orioles relief pitcher-to-be Tim Stoddard moving bodies up front. The rivalry would produce some surreal running and gunning, but Maryland stopped attacking the basket and went to a delay in the closing minutes that gave Thompson some late openings. The first loss at Cole for the junior class of Elmore and McMillen came on an improbable put-back by Thompson that gave him 37 points and the Wolfpack an 87-85 victory.

"Joe Cafferky took a jumper on the wing, and against any other team we get the rebound," Howard said. "Bob Bodell boxed out Thompson, did everything the right way. He faced the basket, located Thompson's body, widened his stance, and blocked out perfectly. Thompson went right above him and it wasn't even a tap. He grabbed the miss and set the ball back down through the basket. I can remember this roar at Cole Field House becoming a hush. The place is so quiet, you can hear a rat take a leak on a cotton ball."

Thompson continued to quiet Maryland. State won the rematch in Raleigh and the ACC final by two as Elmore sat out to rest a foot injury, a logical precaution. With the Wolfpack on probation for recruiting violations, a semifinal win over Wake Forest earned Maryland its first NCAA berth in 15 years. The Terps whipped Syracuse, 91-75, in the Sweet 16, their tournament opener, but were disposed of by a rugged Providence team, 103-89, in the East Region final. The Friars made Maryland and the ACC look tame. Ernie DiGregorio, whose ball-handling repertoire included half-court, behind-the-back passes, walked up to Bodell and said, "You're the D? I'm the D." Jim Barnes had already taken the nickname "Bad News," but Marvin Barnes roughed up McMillen.

"On an in-bounds play, Mac was guarding Marvin Barnes," Roy said. "I smacked Barnes from behind and stepped back. Unfortunately for Mac, Barnes turned around and slapped him. I got to play with Barnes on the St. Louis Spirits in the old ABA. He had a lot of talent, but he played to a different drummer."

The sanctions against N.C. State were lifted for the 1973–74 season, one of the ACC's most memorable. The campaign began with an Associated Press top five of UCLA, N.C. State, Indiana, Maryland, and North Carolina. There was one huge catch: only the conference tournament champion would go to the NCAAs, which was still limited to a 25-team field that consisted of league titlists and a few independents.

It would be six years before expansion would bring in Georgia Tech, and the ACC had only seven members. The regular season champion played only two games in the tournament, so seeding consideration raised the stakes in January and February. Maryland's anxiety started early, as Driesell obsessed over a December 1 opener at defending NCAA

North Carolina State's David Thompson soared above the crowd in the ACC and ruined Super Bowl Sunday at Cole in 1973. A year later, he helped end the hopes of one of Maryland's best teams. (Hornbake Library.)

champion UCLA. He scheduled practices on Pacific time, and spent the preseason plotting to take down the front line of Walton, Keith Wilkes, and Dave Meyers. The Terps climbed out of an early hole, but Lucas couldn't break through a double team on the final possession, and UCLA won, 65-64, another instance of Maryland's inability to finish in big games. The Bruins' 88-game winning streak ended January 19 at Notre Dame—which had won the recruiting race for DeMatha's Adrian Dantley—but Maryland came as close as anyone did at Pauley Pavilion to ending that NCAA record run.

Two weeks later in St. Louis, UCLA whipped N.C. State by 18, but the Wolfpack maintained its spell over Maryland. The Terps made another trip to the West Coast for the Cable Car Classic in Oakland, California, but McMillen was distracted by the Rhodes scholarship application process and the death of his father. State took another Super Bowl Sunday show-down with an 80-74 win at Reynolds Coliseum. When the two teams met at Cole on January 30, the Wolfpack's margin of victory again was six points. That followed a Maryland loss at North Carolina, and in effect clinched the regular-season title, top seed, and first-round bye in the ACC tournament for State.

College basketball was given a classic on March 2, when North Carolina came from eight points down in the final 17 seconds, caught Duke, and won in overtime. Within a week it lost some of its cachet, how-ever, as second-seeded Maryland and N.C. State were on a collision course at the Greensboro Coliseum. Maryland handled Duke by 19 in the first round of the ACC tournament and North Carolina by 20 in the semi-finals. N.C. State, seeded first with an unbeaten conference record for the second straight year—it would be a decade before Jordan and North Carolina gave the ACC another perfect regular season—ran past Virginia by 21 in the other semifinal.

The Wolfpack was coached by Norm Sloan, whose plaids made Driesell's wardrobe seem reserved. Sloan goaded Burleson with the all-ACC team, which gave the nod to Elmore, and a quote from the Terp that maintained he was the best center in the conference. Elmore shakes his head at any suggestion that an elimination game wasn't motivation enough, but Burleson cited the pecking order as inspiration for his 38 points in the title game, when he made 18 of his 25 field-goal attempts. At the time, college basketball—and even the pro game—was downright dainty compared with the contact that is condoned in the new millen-nium, and Elmore and Roy would thrive throwing their weight around today. Watch a game from the 1970s on ESPN Classic, and you won't see the hand-checking and holding that have lowered shooting percentages.

It was simply harder to defend in 1974; there were few stops, and turnovers were a rumor in the ACC final.

Maryland hit 12 of its first 14 shots, and led 25-12 after six minutes. State warmed up and trimmed the difference to 55-50 at the half, as all of that gaudy offensive talent ran up and down the floor unimpeded. N.C. State had a 97-93 lead with a little more than two minutes left, but baskets by Roy and Elmore forced a tie. With Towe cramping on the bench, the Terps stripped his replacement and had the ball at the end of regulation play. Momentarily open on the baseline, Howard decided against shooting over Burleson and passed back to Lucas, who rushed a long jumper that was way off the mark. Howard's free throw gave the Terps their last lead at 100-99, but they had little left in their tank in the overtime, as Lucas missed a one and one and Phil Spence put State on top for good en route to a 103-100 victory.

McMillen later howled about the inequities of Tobacco Road, but at least he didn't have to play the tournament at Reynolds Coliseum, as his brother Jay had. Roy said, "Lefty was not one to substitute unless you died or fouled out," and for the second straight day Driesell called only two reserves off a bench that had been thinned by transfers. Whatever the alibis, Maryland became the only team ever to lose three straight ACC tournament championship games, and there is no doubt that the 1973–74 Terps were the best team never to play in the NCAA tournament.

Driesell grew impatient with ACC officials who wanted the Terps to stay on the court for the postgame awards, but later he climbed aboard the N.C. State bus and wished the Wolfpack well. It avenged its only loss of the season in the NCAA semifinals, where N.C. State dethroned UCLA. The NCAA final was anticlimactic, as the Wolfpack beat Marquette and gave the ACC its only national champion from 1958 to 1981. Having been there and done that, Maryland turned down the NIT and finished with a 23-5 record.

Later that year, the NCAA expanded its tournament to more than one team per conference. In the 1976 tournament, Indiana stopped Michigan in an all–Big Ten final; within a decade the NCAA tournament grew from 25 to 64 teams. That expansion transformed the ACC tournament from an intense event that elicited emotion bordering on religious hysteria to a cozy reunion that seems more like a four-day cocktail party for boosters.

"You talk about pressure, that was pressure," Driesell said. "I think it was a factor in UCLA's winning all them NCAA titles. They didn't have a tournament. If you won three games in that ACC tournament, you were wrung out. That's when the ACC tournament really had some meaning. Right now, it's just a fund-raiser. It's still exciting, but it's not like it used to be."

10

DELIVERING DOUBLE-FIGURE SCORING in 74 straight games, Tom McMillen had been automatic. He left Maryland in 1974 as its all-time leader in points, 1,807, and his career scoring average of 20.5 is a school record that may never be broken. Had McMillen come along two years later, after the NCAA ban on freshmen playing varsity had been lifted, the Terp scoring record might be in the vicinity of 2,400 points. Len Elmore still holds every Maryland rebounding mark, and his career total of 1,053 was also accumulated in just three seasons. These two players were the Terps' greatest inside combination ever, but their legacy in the NCAA tournament consisted of one victory.

Elmore and McMillen graduated in 1974, but coach Lefty Driesell quickly restocked his roster when Maryland signed Moses Malone of Petersburg, Virginia. He would have been one of the best big men in the nation, and would have been teamed with the one of the slickest guards, Lucas. Those plans unraveled when Malone turned pro, however, and one other factor lessened the pressure on the Terps. Before Malone broke Driesell's heart with his groundbreaking jump to the pros, the NCAA mollified Driesell and dozens of other coaches with the announcement that it was opening its tournament to more than one team per conference. It was a season too late for what had been the best Maryland team to that time. Expectations were lowered, but only a bit, and the 1974–75 Terps exceeded them with an interesting mix that included a future Olympian, two brawny big men, and a three-guard lineup. If it wasn't the best team that had performed at Cole Field House, at the least it was the most entertaining.

Maryland had been so top-heavy with big men that Driesell hadn't known what to do in previous seasons with players like Tom Roy and Owen Brown, who were 6-foot-9. Driesell had tinkered with towering lineups that had proved too plodding, and now he faced a different problem. He didn't have enough bodies to bang inside, but neither did anyone else in college basketball, as the consensus All-America team from the previous season had included three senior centers, UCLA's Bill Walton, Providence's Marvin Barnes, and Notre Dame's John Shumate. Driesell had lost two great low post players in Elmore and Malone, the man-child who had been supposed to replace him, but his backcourt was well stocked.

Lucas was simply the best guard in the nation. Mo Howard was eager to see what he could produce getting more than nine shots per game, and there was a freshman just as talented as those two juniors. Playing against Malone, some of the Washington Bullets, and other pros in the Urban Coalition League, Brad Davis had held his own in the summer of 1974, and it was obvious that he wasn't going to require a lengthy apprenticeship off the bench. Similar in size and build to Lucas, Davis had a quick, rangy frame and was also a gifted two-sport athlete. Drafted by the Pittsburgh Pirates, Davis had averaged 14.2 rebounds for his high school team in Monaca, Pennsylvania, but he was better suited to run a fast break than to start one.

Driesell experimented with a three-guard lineup in a preseason tournament in Mexico. When Lucas suffered a broken collarbone in the opener against Richmond and missed five games, Davis took over at the point and doubled the number of starters with zero college experience. Steve Sheppard, a powerful 6-6 sophomore from the Bronx, New York, who had sat out the previous season for academic reasons, settled into the small forward spot. When Lucas returned, Davis returned to the sixth-man role, to the chagrin of teammates who thought the Terps operated better with the freshman at the point.

"Out goes Luke and in comes Brad, rocking and rolling and kicking people's butts," Roy said. "Brad was a freshman, wet behind the ears, but it was funny, the way he made you pay for not looking at him. In practice, when you went through the middle, if you weren't looking, you were going to get hit in the head. Luke comes back, and we lose to UCLA. I'm not blaming Luke, but we had kismet, we had a rotation going. With Luke, when you have somebody that talented, the tendency is for the ball to be in his hands. Luke was a shooting point guard. Brad was the person who took us to another gear. I took the ball out of bounds, and by the time I took two steps onto the floor, they were shooting. On most of our possessions, I never got to half court. With three guards, if they got into a rhythm, there wasn't any keeping up with them."

In the late 1980s, Paul Westhead would be acclaimed as an offensive innovator when Loyola Marymount took NCAA scoring records to new levels with his offense that called for minimal time of possession and for three-point attempts off the fast break. The 1971 slowdown against South Carolina was a signature win for Driesell, but he preferred getting his shooters open with a torrid pace. In 1964, his fourth Davidson team had set an NCAA record for field-goal percentage, .544. Eleven years later, with Davis's foot on the accelerator and Lucas as proficient as ever running the break, another Driesell team established a new NCAA record, as Maryland shot .547 from the field.

The 1974–75 Terps still rank as the second-best shooting team in ACC history. Two scrubs were the only players who shot below 50 percent. Maryland averaged 89.9 points a game, still a school record. From Lucas's 19.5 to Roy's 11.0, the team had an astounding six players average in double-figure scoring.

Minus Lucas, Maryland went with a traditional look in early December that had Owen Brown, Roy, and Sheppard on the front line, but Lucas came back just in time for a December 28 game that took on historic proportions at the end of the season. In what turned out to be the last game he coached on the East Coast, John Wooden got an 81-75 victory out of No. 3 UCLA at the expense of the fifth-ranked Terps in the championship game of the Maryland Invitational Tournament. At the 1975 Final Four in San Diego, Wooden announced that he was retiring, and the Bruins predictably picked up his 10th NCAA championship in 12 seasons. Three months earlier at Cole, Wooden had exposed the match-up problems that

Lefty Driesell had an abundance of perimeter talent in the 1974–75 season, when he finally went to a three-guard lineup. Brad Davis, Mo Howard, Billy Hahn, and John Lucas (left to right) headed up court on media day. (News American collection.)

would face the Terps, as the 6-3 Howard was just too slight to stop 6-6 Marques Johnson, UCLA's not-so-small forward.

Three weeks later at Cole, Maryland ended a six-game losing streak to N.C. State and Thompson. The Terps didn't lose again until January 22, when upstart Clemson knocked them off. Back home at Cole, they lost again when they couldn't score for nine minutes against North Carolina and Dean Smith's four-corner offense. Maryland ran wild in February, however, as it swept its last nine regular-season games and gave the program its first ACC regular-season championship, with a 10-2 record.

A remarkable succession of Saturdays in February began with a battle in Raleigh. Shaking up his team after the complacent losses to Clemson and North Carolina, Driesell benched Sheppard and started the three guards for the first time, and the Terps ended the Wolfpack's 37-game winning streak at Reynolds Coliseum. Lucas picked up his fourth foul with nearly 15 minutes left and Roy was ejected with six remaining, but Howard broke loose for a career-high 29 points and Davis became a 40-minute man. He never came out, and his short-runner over DeMatha grad Kenny Carr was the difference in a 98-97 win.

Maryland won at all four Tobacco Road schools that season. In December, it pounded Wake Forest by 21. Bolstered by the clutch victory at State, the Terps rolled by 24 at Duke and 22 at North Carolina, their first win ever at Carmichael Auditorium, the home of the Tar Heels from 1965 to January 1986. Maryland clinched the regular-season title and the top seed in the ACC tournament with a 70-64 victory at Cole over Clemson. In Skip Wise, the only freshman named all-ACC before 1990, the Tigers had maybe the most talented player ever out of Baltimore, but Roy outplayed 7-1 Tree Rollins.

Thompson got his revenge in the semifinals of the ACC tournament in Greensboro, where N.C. State beat a seemingly uninterested Maryland team by two. North Carolina upset the Wolfpack in the ACC final to begin the Tar Heels' record run of 27 straight appearances in the NCAA tournament, and the Terps were rewarded for their season's work with a favorable bracket in the Midwest Region.

Maryland entered the 1975 NCAA tournament ranked fourth in the nation. No. 1 Indiana didn't fare well, as Scott May's broken arm helped Kentucky beat the Hoosiers in a regional final, the round where Maryland's season ended, too. The Terps beat Creighton in Lubbock, Texas, and then met Notre Dame in Las Cruces, New Mexico, where Adrian Dantley outscored Lucas but the Terps won, 83-71.

For the second time in three seasons and the fourth time in eight, a Driesell team was stopped one game shy of the Final Four. Louisville coach Denny Crum, a former assistant of Wooden's at UCLA, didn't have anyone like Lucas, but the Cardinals had an assortment of rugged perimeter players. Crum inverted his offense, and his guards posted up Maryland's. Davis couldn't keep up with Philip Bond at the point, and Louisville cruised to a 96-82 victory. At the Final Four, the Cardinals lost their semifinal by one to UCLA, and the Bruins then beat Kentucky, despite 34 points by Kevin Grevey.

Throughout the nation, basketball fans paid homage to Wooden, and the Wizard of Westwood graced Maryland's team banquet. In College Park, there was appreciation for a very wild bunch. That Maryland team was freewheeling on the court and off. The Vietnam War was over, tensions had lessened on campus, and the 1974–75 Terps lived for the provocative statement and majored in fun. Moses Malone may not have shown up at Cole Field House in September 1974, but Elvis Presley did for a two-night run, and the Terps made sure they were in attendance. "Any guy who has women throwing panties at him," Howard said, "we wanted to see what he's doing."

Lucas led the loose Terps. It was Lefty's team, but it was Luke's world. He invited references to *Cool Hand Luke,* a 1967 chain-gang drama, but while Lucas could match Paul Newman's insouciance, Richard Roundtree was his cinema role model. Lucas went through his "Shaft" phase. He might not have been much for breaking bad with men who crossed his path, but he liked the part of the image that had him surrounded by women.

Mike Douchant's encyclopedia of college basketball placed Lucas on a ten-man all-1970s team, a group that included Larry Bird, Magic Johnson, David Thompson, and Bill Walton. He left Maryland with career records for points, 2,015, and assists, 514, and he was the only one who was a world-class athlete in two sports. While Dick Drescher, who had played basketball for the Terps from 1965 to 1968, nearly earned a spot in the 1976 Olympics in the discus, the argument over the best athlete ever at Maryland usually comes down to Lucas and Renaldo Nehemiah, who held the world record in the 110-meter hurdles from 1979 to 1989 and played wide receiver for the San Francisco 49ers.

A junior Davis Cup player, Lucas could get to returns, and he had an assortment of dangerous serves. Roscoe Tanner was in a class of his own when it came to cranking a first serve in the 1970s, but Lucas generated as much speed as nearly anyone else in the world. Had Lucas devoted himself to tennis, Jimmy Connors and John McEnroe might have had another serious challenger, and one equally quotable.

John Lucas held court wherever he went. Trainer J. J. Bush, who arrived at Maryland in 1972, the same year as Lucas, readied him for practice as Mike Cherry and Brad Davis looked on. (Maryland Sports Information.)

Lucas moved from basketball to tennis and back on his own terms. Driesell prohibited him from playing tennis during basketball season, but he would sneak into Ritchie Coliseum, play pick-up basketball for use of the floor, then roll out a makeshift tennis court and volley. He paid Driesell back by detouring the Terp tennis team through Petersburg, Virginia, on ACC road trips. As his teammates fretted about being in a bad neighborhood, Lucas talked up Malone. David Pessin, a tennis teammate who became the legal representative of 1990s Maryland hero Walt Williams, saw Lucas as a charismatic figure. Pampered by his parents, Lucas knew what his fame allowed him to get away with.

"We were a fairly eclectic crowd, and we did our very best to keep John in check," Pessin said of the tennis team. "Doyle Royal was the coach, and John used to ask him, 'What's your middle name, Poyle?' John went out of his way to say the most outrageous things. He was going to be the first black president. When he played World Team Tennis, his mixed doubles partner was Renee Richards, a transsexual who had been a pretty good men's player out of the East, Richard Raskin. John used to say, 'Hit the ball, Dick.' John was bigger than life. We ran out of gas driving through Durham once. John got out and before he could wave his arms, the first car stopped. After hours, whenever we got hungry, Luke's room was the place to go. People were always sending him cakes, pies. We all had little refrigerators in our dorm rooms. John had a full-sized one."

While Lucas was out on the town, Sheppard stayed in his room and did sit-ups in bed. The crowds at Cole didn't know what to make of Roy,

who did not seek their approval. They booed him when he played miserably on January 2, against Appalachian State. Two days later, when his defense helped beat Dantley and Notre Dame, there were cheers for Roy, who showed he wasn't that fickle.

"Against Appalachian State, I got three quick fouls, played horrible, and fouled out," Roy said. "There was booing from the student section, so I made a gesture. The next game we played, I guarded Dantley, did a pretty good job, and got a standing ovation. I gave them the same signal. They went wild."

Was that gesture his middle finger?

"Yeah," Roy said.

In February, Roy was ejected at N.C. State. In January, Brown was tossed from the Wake Forest win at Cole for fighting. He fancied himself the biggest, baddest Terp of all, but one day Driesell showed him what a bald man in his 40s was capable of.

The NCAA wrestling championships were conducted at Cole five times, which heightened Driesell's running territorial war with Terp coach Sully Krouse. One day a wrestler with an injured hand did his condition-

The gold medal team at the 1976 Olympics included Steve Sheppard (middle player, front row) and luminaries like coach Dean Smith (front row, far left); Adrian Dantley (front row, second player from left); Phil Ford (front row, far right); and assistant coach John Thompson (second row, far left). (Maryland Sports Information.)

ing on the concourse, the ten-foot-wide cement walkway that was five and one-third laps to a mile. Driesell complained that the privacy of his practice had been breached. The next day, Krouse sent his entire team to run on the concourse. Wrestling mats on the court irked Driesell, who, unbeknownst to his players, knew a little about the sport. After all, Granby High in Norfolk, Virginia, was the home of the Granby Roll, and Driesell twice pinned Brown as they horsed around before practice one day.

"Hey, I went to Granby High," Driesell said. "The coach was Billy Martin, probably the greatest wrestling coach in America. He invented the Granby Roll, I just knew how to do that. I remember doing it to Owen. I told him I was going to take bottom, and I pinned him. Then I took top and pinned him again. He was always going on."

Driesell went from laughing with Brown to weeping over him in 1976, the hardest year of his coaching career until 1986. Both ordeals involved the deaths of young players, and during the Bicentennial year, Driesell had to endure a double dose of tragedy.

Brown was a senior in 1974–75, when the freshman class that featured Davis also included Chris Patton. Both were 6-9, but had little else in common. Brown, from La Grange, Illinois, averaged 14.9 points and helped Roy do the dirty work under the basket. Born in Bessemer, Alabama, Patton had played his high school ball in New York. A *Parade* All-American, Patton had developed his ball-handling skills because he was painfully thin and not physically ready for the ACC wars. An assortment of ailments kept him out of ten games in his freshman season.

Patton's development continued during the 1975–76 season, when Brown and Roy moved on and their spots in the rotation were filled by Lawrence Boston, a transfer from junior-college power Vincennes, and Larry Gibson, a freshman from Baltimore's Dunbar High. Maryland had a 13-2 record when Gibson busted up a knee at North Carolina on January 25, 1976. The Terps lost in overtime, and the rest of the season went down from there.

The Terps didn't even make the NCAA tournament, despite a 22-6 record and a national ranking of No. 12. With the ACC tournament finally pried loose from Tobacco Road and in Maryland's backyard at the Capital Centre, the Terps lost to Virginia in the semifinals of the ACC tournament. Their 7-5 record in the conference didn't warrant the league's at-large bid, which went to regular-season champion North Carolina. Basketball had lost some of its meaning anyway. Less than a year removed from helping the Terps get within a win of their first Final Four, Owen Brown died on February 4, 1976.

Brown had taken his diploma to the Xerox corporate training center in Leesburg, Virginia. On the same day the Terps won in Charlottesville, he collapsed during a pick-up game and died of a heart attack brought on by hypertropic cardiomyopathy. Some of his former teammates still can't grasp the news that awaited them when they got back to College Park.

"I hit some free throws at the end of the game at Virginia," Howard said. "We were on Route 66 returning to campus, and I can remember a car on the other side of the highway, with its lights flashing. In my mind, somebody went out there to try to stop our bus. We got back to the dorm, on the sixth floor of Ellicott Hall, and Luke said, 'Somebody just called me and asked if I had heard about Owen Brown.' I said, 'That's a dumb joke.' I know he was listening to that game on the radio. I expected to talk to him that night about the game, but I never got the chance.

"Owen was an only child, and after he died, his mom would call and ask the most penetrating questions. Her heart was broken, and so was mine. Tom McMillen was a Rhodes scholar. Owen Brown could have been, but he wanted something else. Owen was my roommate for two years, and he helped me grow a lot. A higher power matched me up with him so I could learn about life. My oldest son is named Ashley Owen Howard. When he was born, I didn't think of naming him anything other than Owen. We were so close, they called us 'Mowen.' For a man to say he loves another man is hard to do. Owen was the first man outside my family I said that to."

The Houston Rockets took Lucas with the No. 1 selection in the NBA draft that summer. Sheppard was chosen for the U.S. Olympic team and won a gold medal in Montreal. A cloud, however, remained over College Park. On April 1, two days before he was to play in a Heart Fund tournament in the memory of Brown, Patton collapsed on the courts on the Byrd Stadium concourse. Brown had played for Maryland despite an irregular heartbeat. Patton, who suffered from Marfan's syndrome, never recovered from a ruptured aorta. He was 21.

"When you thought you could stand, you were bent over again," Howard said. "I will never forget the two of them pulling pranks in the locker room and then going against each other in practice. Those two guys were ahead of their time. Today, they'd be Kevin Garnett. When you're young, and you've gone through the same hell that Lefty has put you through, that keeps you connected. You're 19, 20, 21 and away from home for the first time, and those guys become your family. They were the best substitute family I ever had."

When Gary Williams showed his distress during a shocking loss at Cole to Florida State on February 14, 2001, he had no idea that Maryland was about to turn its season around and barge into its first Final Four. (Baltimore Sun.)

Point guard Steve Blake celebrated a win at No. 2 Duke by leaping into the arms of senior reserve center Mike Mardesich. The upset came 13 days after Maryland's desultory loss
to Florida State. (Associated Press.)

Byron Mouton transferred in from Tulane and perked up the Terps with his effervescent play. This fist pump came after his pivotal basket against Georgetown, in a win that put Gary Williams in the Elite Eight for the first time. (Baltimore Sun.)

Lonny Baxter was devastated when he was called for his fifth foul against Duke in the 2001 NCAA semifinals. Maryland's first trip to the Final Four unraveled in a foul-plagued semifinal loss to the Blue Devils. (Baltimore Sun.)

Duke's Jason Williams (left) was the consensus national player of the year in 2001–2002, but Juan Dixon (right) was the ACC Player of the Year and performed best when it counted the most. (Baltimore Sun.)

Teammate Byron Mouton (1) and Duke center Carlos Boozer admire a dunk by Chris Wilcox, who began his sophomore season as a reserve but emerged as one of the nation's best big men with a game that downed the Blue Devils in their final visit to Cole. (Baltimore Sun.)

Tom McMillen (holding ball) was among the former Terp greats who helped close Cole on March 3, 2002. A ball-passing ceremony followed a 20-point blowout of Virginia, which had also been Maryland's first victim there in 1955. (Baltimore Sun.)

Juan Dixon strips Wisconsin's Travon Davis in the second round of the 2002 NCAA tournament. Dixon was more than a clutch shooter; in ACC history only Johnny Rhodes, another former Maryland star, had bettered his 333 career steals. (Baltimore Sun.)

A deep, physical front line strengthened Maryland throughout the 2001–2002 season. In the Sweet 16 win over Kentucky, reserve Ryan Randle made his presence known to Jules Camara. (Baltimore Sun.)

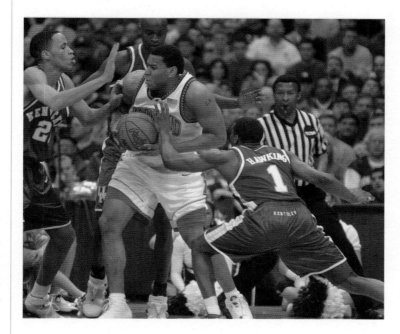

Lonny Baxter posed match-up problems for most opponents. He drew a crowd against Kentucky, but still managed 16 points in a performance that helped him to East Regional MVP honors. (Baltimore Sun.)

Maryland veterans, including Gary Williams, contend that Juan Dixon's long three-pointer over Connecticut's Taliek Brown in the East Regional final was the biggest clutch shot in Maryland history. (Baltimore Sun.)

Indiana fans outnumbered Maryland's at the 2002 Final Four at the Georgia Dome, but these students from First Baptist Church in Springfield, Virginia, were there to cheer on the Terps. (Baltimore Sun.)

Guard Drew Nicholas took to the floor, literally, as he and Juan Dixon double-teamed Kansas's Nick Collison in the NCAA semifinals. The willingness of reserves like Nicholas to accept a role gave Maryland a strong rotation of players. (Baltimore Sun.)

Juan Dixon and Gary Williams were loose at Maryland's practice before the NCAA semifinals. They enjoyed a unique relationship, as the coach understood the family dysfunction that had marked his star player's upbringing. (Associated Press.)

Point guard Steve Blake eluded Indiana's Tom Coverdale (3) and Jared Jeffries in the NCAA final. Blake had only one assist in the second half, but that pivotal feed to Juan Dixon put Maryland on top for good. (Baltimore Sun.)

Half of Indiana's 20 baskets in the NCAA final came on three-pointers; Lonny Baxter's block of Jared Jeffries was indicative of the defensive work that brought Maryland its first NCAA championship. (Baltimore Sun.)

Juan Dixon was draped in a net and Gary Williams was drained as Maryland soaked up the adulation of its fans after the Terps beat Indiana 64-52 to complete their climb to the top of college basketball. (Baltimore Sun.)

THE YEAR 1977 WAS BITTERSWEET for Lefty Driesell. For the first time since 1971, his Terps failed to get past the first round of the Atlantic Coast Conference tournament. There were reports that four of his players were on shaky academic ground. Talent left and talent came, as Brad Davis cut short his relationship with a coach he had never gotten along with, but three scorers arrived. When they were joined by a big man named Buck who specialized in dirty work, Driesell had the makings of a team that would bring Maryland an unexpected ACC regular-season championship.

Instead of being Moses Malone's junior season, 1976–77 became one to forget. Larry Gibson gallantly came back from a busted kneecap, but Olympic gold medalist Steve Sheppard suffered an Achilles tendon injury, and both played through pain and a drop in production. Even Driesell hurt his Achilles. After the Terps meekly lost to N.C. State to finish a 19-8 season, they had to stomach North Carolina's winning the NCAA's East Regional at Cole Field House.

Davis followed the lead of his brother Mickey, who had left Duquesne early to play in the American Basketball Association, and filed for the NBA draft. The junior guard, whose 431 career assists had been bettered only by John Lucas, was taken with the 15th selection by the Los Angeles Lakers. Maryland was left with Gibson, 6-8 Lawrence Boston, and a young, thin backcourt after Brian Magid and Turkey Tillman transferred out, but help was on the way.

Greg Manning, a sharp 6-foot-1 guard with fine fundamental skills, came from a small Pennsylvania town south of Harrisburg. Wearing the 25 of Gus Johnson but with a game that also seemed inspired by Earl Monroe, another star from the Baltimore Bullets, 6-7 forward Ernie Graham was the best player in a big city.

Albert King had starred in the biggest city of all. Before his precocious body and skills piled up gaudy numbers for Fort Hamilton High School, the 6-6 King had been a 14-year-old legend in New York. King's commitment lessened the knock that Driesell had lost his recruiting touch. There might have been less pressure on the coach, but it rarely eased up on his

Ernie Graham, shooting over Virginia's Ralph Sampson, was a complete offensive player. He set the school single-game scoring record as a sophomore, then led the Terps in assists as a junior and senior. (News American collection.)

biggest recruit since Tom McMillen. King usually dealt with the curiosity by staying in his dorm room and listening to music.

"When I was 14, I didn't understand what was going on," said King, who had a nine-year NBA career and then purchased a couple of fast-food franchises. "I tried to hide from the experience. I got frustrated by all of the attention, because when I was young, I was an introvert. My personality is totally different now, and I would tell most people to enjoy the experience. I got to be in *Sports Illustrated,* and travel the world. People come up to me to talk about *Heaven Is a Playground,* and I have to laugh. That made me known, but with cable and ESPN and the Internet, now those kinds of expectations are placed on more kids."

As King acclimated to College Park, the *Diamondback* and the now-defunct *Washington Star* reported on the academic probation of Gibson, John Bilney, and two sophomore guards from Washington, D.C., Bill Bryant and Jo Jo Hunter. The four filed a lawsuit over invasion of privacy that was dismissed in 1978, and Driesell dealt with speculation that all four were in danger of dismissal from the university. His antagonistic relationship with the media intensified, and there was rancor in the Terps' ranks, too.

"We were loaded with talent, but sometimes you can have too much," Manning said of the 1977–78 season. "I remember that we didn't have great chemistry. Bryant and Hunter were best friends, and when one wasn't playing, things got uneasy. I'll never forget walking around the concourse on Byrd Stadium, on my way back to my dorm after practice one day. It was about three weeks into practice. One of them said, 'You're young, you're never going to play here. You might want to think about transferring.' I was naïve, but I wanted to play and start. I turned around and said, 'I hope you're real good friends. One of you isn't going to be playing, because I have one of the guard spots.' From that point on, we didn't have a real good relationship. I wouldn't say it was class warfare, but there was unrest on that team. The average person just doesn't understand how competitive the fight for playing time can become."

By December, Manning had joined King in the starting lineup. Boston's 15.5 average led the Terps in scoring. King showed the quickest second jump on the offensive boards that anyone had ever seen in College Park. Manning, who was used to shooting at Steelton-Highspire High, had to run the point and received an education in an ACC that included Phil Ford at North Carolina, Clyde Austin at N.C. State, and a Duke team that reached the NCAA final. The Terps went 3-9 in the ACC, Driesell's worst conference record ever, and barely broke even overall with a 15-13 record.

Bryant and Hunter eventually transferred elsewhere, but the backcourt was replenished with two capable point guards. Philadelphia's Reggie Jackson thought shoot first. DeMatha's Dutch Morley was a more traditional floor general. But they were not the biggest catches in the recruiting class that arrived in 1978.

Buck Williams was listed at 6-8 and 215 pounds, but played as if he was so much bigger. Like Manning, he hailed from small-town USA, and he brought solid skills and a ferocious competitiveness up from Rocky Mount, North Carolina. More than two decades later, Driesell said he still hadn't coached a more intense player. Defense, relentless rebounding, and an ability to set bone-jarring screens enabled Williams to spend 17 seasons in the NBA and have his number retired by the New Jersey Nets. He knew how to go to the glass and clean it the day he walked into Cole, and Williams's rebounding average of 10.8 in 1978–79 has been bettered by only one other Terp rookie, Len Elmore.

A changing of the guard in the Washington area didn't bode well for the ACC and Maryland in 1978–79, when the Terps lost to Georgetown for the first time since Driesell's second season. North Carolina and Duke were the top seeds in the East Region, but lost their NCAA tournament openers in Raleigh to Pennsylvania and St. John's, respectively, in what came to be known as Black Friday on Tobacco Road. Their presence would not have mattered at the Final Four, where Magic Johnson and Larry Bird elevated the college game to an unprecedented level of awareness in the Michigan State–Indiana State final.

Two days after that clash of the titans, Manning followed frightening news unfolding from his Pennsylvania hometown, as America's worst nuclear accident at a commercial power plant unfolded at nearby Three Mile Island.

Maryland went 19-11 that season, which ended with a loss to Ohio State in the second round of the National Invitation Tournament. The most memorable wins featured players from Baltimore's Dunbar, Gibson and Graham.

Graham was a revelation, as he led the Terps in scoring with a 16.6 average. The biggest night of his career came on December 20, 1978. N.C. State came to Cole with a No. 4 ranking, but everyone left talking about Graham.

"As the players were shooting around before the game, the horn sounded and Ernie ran after a ball that was going out of bounds in the corner," said Billy Packer, the television analyst that night. "Ernie grabbed the ball as he was falling out of bounds, took a turnaround jumper that went over the corner of the backboard and went swish. Our broadcast began, and in our opening comments, I said, 'Ernie Graham is going to be out of sight tonight.' I can remember that shot like it happened ten minutes ago, but I wasn't looking for anything that spectacular out of him. I just needed an opening."

Graham provided the closing. Slowed by early foul trouble, he poured in 30 points in the second half and finished with a school-record 44. Toward the end of a 124-110 victory over the Wolfpack that remains the highest-scoring ACC game ever, Graham couldn't miss. Had there been a three-point line, he might have finished with 50.

"I remember one shot he hit in the second half, across from our bench," Manning said. "He was falling out of bounds, and he buries one. As only Ernie could do, he slowly gets up and uses that unique gait, lumbering down the floor. Every time he touched the ball, the crowd went crazy. State was switching men on him, denying him the ball, but Ernie was talented and knew how to get off his shot. He was big and he could stroke it, and they just couldn't stop him. We had guys who could score a ton, but what made us dangerous was that we could distribute the ball."

Five weeks after Graham's big game, Manning's pass to Gibson led to a three-point play and a one-point win over top-ranked Notre Dame. Williams outplayed Bill Laimbeer, and Gibson produced the biggest clutch play of a career that alternated between promise and misfortune.

When Gibson was a sophomore at Dunbar High, he had started in the Poets' monumental upset of DeMatha. In December of his senior season, he was stabbed in a disagreement over his stolen leather coat, and missed three games. Driesell still wanted him badly, but a broken kneecap ended his freshman season with the Terps. More modern medicine might have meant a swifter rehabilitation for Gibson, and maybe at least one NCAA berth. Gibson landed in Europe and happily discovered that there is more to pro basketball than the NBA.

Graham and Skip Wise followed and preceded Gibson, respectively, as the stars at Dunbar. Wise was the first freshman to make all-ACC first team, but left Clemson after one season for an ill-advised jump to the ABA. The move didn't work out, and Wise fell into a life that included

Greg Manning was one of the best shooters in Maryland history. His free-throw records have stood for more than two decades, and his field-goal percentage was remarkably high for a guard. (News American collection.)

crime and prison. Graham didn't know how to cope with the fallout from his school scoring record. He was hurt by criticism that he was a gunner, and he had his own drug problems. As Graham told Mike Preston of the *Sun* in 2002, "I know I spent a million easy in drugs during my career." After he was done playing professionally, Graham founded Get the Message, which combines talks about basketball and living drug free. "I've got God in my life now," Graham said. "I did some work down at Maryland, and had some fans love me, too."

Duke, North Carolina, and Virginia, which had won the recruiting war for 7-4 Ralph Sampson, were all ranked in the top 15 heading into the 1979–80 season. Although Gibson was the only player of consequence not returning, Maryland was taken lightly. What followed was maybe the Terps' most satisfying regular season ever. Midway through January, it still wasn't ranked in the Top 20, but Maryland went 11-3 in the conference and became just the second Terp team to finish atop the ACC regular-season standings.

King averaged 21.7 points, made 55.3 percent of his shots, and became the first Terp to be named ACC Player of the Year. No Maryland player on a winning team had scored as much since Gene Shue, in 1953–54. Manning was the nation's fourth-best free-throw shooter, but, more significant, he was sixth in field-goal accuracy, which is customarily dominated by players who operate close to the basket. Manning stood out wherever he went, as he became the first Terp since Tom McMillen to be named Academic All-American. Graham led with 136 assists, the most ever by a Maryland player who wasn't running the point. Williams gave the Terps a fourth player averaging over 15 points, and that combination was potent on January 20, 1980. With the Tar Heels' James Worthy out with a broken foot, Driesell got only his second win at North Carolina's Carmichael Auditorium, as King collected 28 points, Williams 19, Graham 17, and Manning 16. If only that season could have ended in February.

Maryland fought off Georgia Tech and Clemson to reach its first ACC tournament final since the loss to N.C. State in the 1974 classic. Duke took a 73-72 lead into the closing seconds, but Williams was in position and poised to put in a miss by King and give the Terps their first official ACC championship in 22 years. Then Kenny Dennard, the power forward on a Blue Devils front line that included Mike Gminski and Gene Banks, undercut Williams and the game was over. Impartial observers must have sympathized, as King was voted Most Valuable Player of the tournament. He put on a marvelous shooting display, as he made 35 of his 53 field-

In some ways, Albert King was even better known than Tom McMillen when they arrived as freshmen. The Terps' first ACC Player of the Year, King improved McMillen's career scoring record. (News American collection.)

goal attempts and poured in 81 points. The only other year in which the champion hadn't produced the MVP or a co-MVP had been 1954, in the first ACC tournament.

"I'm 42 years old, and sometimes when I'm stuck in traffic, my mind wanders and I wonder why that shot didn't go in," King said. "I got the ball to the left of the key and had a good look from a place I liked to shoot, but I guess the rims weren't as soft as I thought. If my shot had went in, then Buck wouldn't have had to rebound. The picture of him getting decked by Dennard tells a thousand words. I didn't want to be bothered with a [MVP] trophy, and I remain in debt to Jack Zane for coaxing me out of the locker room to accept it."

It could be a testy Terp bunch. North Carolina coach Dean Smith's desire to project a classy demeanor included extending a hand to fallen opponents. Driesell warned his players not to let them "kill you with kindness," and Bilney swears he remembers assistant Tom Abatemarco telling Tar Heel counterpart Eddie Fogler to do something anatomically impossible as the North Carolina staff tried to exchange pregame pleasantries. There were none when Maryland, minus the injured Williams, lost to Georgetown in the third game of the season, when Driesell and Hoya coach John Thompson, two men whose physiques could intimidate, had an ugly confrontation in the first half. After Ed Spriggs of the Hoyas received a technical for hanging on the rim, harsh words flew between the coaches. "They weren't anything you could put in a newspaper," Thompson told the media, when asked what he said to Driesell. "I got a little emotional and was telling Lefty he had made the call. The funny thing is I had told my kids not to get emotional, and then I went out and did it."

Maryland opened the NCAA tournament with an 11-point win over Tennessee in Greensboro, then headed to the Spectrum in Philadelphia. Its opponent in the East Sweet 16? Georgetown. Thompson apologized for his language in their earlier game, and Driesell accepted. John Feinstein, then the beat writer for the *Washington Post,* remembers Driesell saying, "To err is human, to forgive divine, and I'm divine." Georgetown won Round Two, 74-68, as Graham was limited to six points, Jackson had a disastrous return to his hometown, and the Hoyas' bench superiority included Eric Smith scoring their last seven points. It would be 14 years before Maryland met Georgetown again.

Brushing aside the defense of North Carolina's Sam Perkins, Buck Williams performed yeoman duty at center despite standing only 6-foot-8. He was the second-best rebounder in Maryland history. (News American collection.)

That Terp team had some curious dynamics. King was the best player in the ACC, but Williams would have gone to the Olympics if President Jimmy Carter had not ordered a boycott of the Moscow Games in retaliation for the Russian invasion of Afghanistan. Jackson and Morley split time at the point, but Graham was the top assist man. As was usually the case, Driesell relied too much on his starters. The late Taylor Baldwin made a nice contribution off the bench, and Bilney likes to think he did, despite rarely leaving it.

"Lefty thought it was best if I give up basketball and concentrate on my studies my senior year," Bilney said. "I was the only guy left from my recruiting class. I wasn't about to quit. I watched my dream go away, but I was OK with it. The other guys weren't interested, but it wasn't hard for me to make suggestions to the coaching staff. Am I not going to get playing time if I do that? I wasn't playing as it was. Lefty always liked to have interaction between his post men, like there was a bar between them. He always had a tandem, whether it was [Tom] McMillen and [Len] Elmore, [Tom] Roy and [Owen] Brown, or Gibson and Boston. He didn't have that when I was a senior, it was Buck and a bunch of shooters. Lefty always had a specific role for people, but he couldn't do that with that team, because all of the parts were interchangeable."

Maryland slipped to fourth in the ACC in 1980–81, despite the return of the entire seven-man rotation and the addition of freshmen Pete Holbert, Steve Rivers, and Herman Veal. It was not a given that King would come back for his senior season, as the Chicago Bulls had floated the offer of a substantial guaranteed contract to coax him into early entry in the NBA draft.

"We were all chasing Albert, trying to find out if he's turning pro," said Feinstein. "He was in hiding. I saw Ernie carrying a boom box, and before I could even get out the question, he said, 'Ask Albert.' I asked him what his problem was. He said, 'My problem is I haven't got Albert's problems.'"

King's preparation for the 1980–81 season was slowed by a chipped foot bone. The Terps' only loss leading up to the ACC campaign came at defending NCAA champion Louisville, but conference play did not go well. Virginia and North Carolina swept Maryland, and the Tar Heels' 76-63 win at Cole on February 15, 1981, was the Terps' worst beating in a conference game there in a decade. There were two constants at Cole for Dean Smith. Until he quit smoking, he would enjoy a cigarette before games with Joe Blair, the loyal Maryland publicist. The hostile noise his teams encountered on the road was usually magnified at Cole, so he couldn't believe what he heard heading into the tunnel at the break. "I think we had them by 20 at the half," Smith said. "They got booed as they went off, and that's the only time I can remember the Maryland fans not being supportive."

Graham and Manning were among the players who questioned the loyalty of the fans. Newspaper columnists argued that the Terps had gone as far as Driesell could take them, and athletic director Jim Kehoe, who had retired in 1978 but returned to the post, acknowledged, "The natives are restless." After Maryland won on the road against a bad N.C. State team, Driesell responded to critics with his famous "I can coach" line. The ACC tournament was back at the Capital Centre, and the pressure to put up or shut up increased.

Maryland got by Duke and rookie coach Mike Krzyzewski in the first round. All of the potential that had made the Terps the No. 4 team in the nation at the start of the season was displayed in the semifinals against Virginia, which had gone 13-1 in ACC regular-season play. Williams set the tone during the introductions, when it looked as if he was trying to slap the hand off Sampson. The National Player of the Year was embarrassed in an 85-62 Maryland romp, while Williams didn't play as if he gave away eight inches. The championship game was business as usual. Days after the publication of a *News American* article in which he had been critical of Driesell, Graham broke free for 27 points on 12-17 shooting. His last basket came on a put-back that got the Terps within a point of North Carolina with four seconds left, but Jimmy Black dribbled out the clock. It was Maryland's fifth loss in the ACC finals in a decade; the last four had been by a combined seven points.

"I'm a religious man, and I don't think the Lord wants me to win this one," Driesell told reporters afterward. "Maybe he wants me to win the national title."

That was wishful thinking. College basketball's sophomore class was loaded in 1980–81. The Terps had played Sampson and North Carolina's James Worthy. They knew about Georgia's Dominique Wilkins and Kentucky's Sam Bowie, and they can't forget their encounter with the slightest-built star in that class. Sixth-seeded Maryland opened the NCAA tournament with a 12-point win over Tennessee-Chattanooga, but had an uneven start to its second-round game in Dayton. Williams was called for two fouls in the first three minutes, but Graham hit a long jumper that gave the Terps a big early lead. On the Indiana bench, Bob Knight didn't flinch. The Hoosiers and Isiah Thomas, who had 14 assists, rolled to a 99-64 rout that was Maryland's worst postseason loss ever. Hours after a would-be assassin shot President Ronald Reagan, the Hoosiers completed their conquest of the NCAA tournament.

It was not a fitting exit for the senior class. King left Maryland with a school-record 2,058 points. Graham collected 1,607 points and 346 assists, a total that had been bettered only by John Lucas and Brad Davis. Manning was the second-best free-throw shooter in ACC history, and his 1,561 points were the fifth-most ever at Maryland. After three hard seasons in college basketball, Williams jumped into the NBA draft early.

Driesell was left with another talent void. It would be filled very close to College Park.

12

BEFORE JUAN DIXON TOOK MARYLAND to unprecedented national heights, there was the late Len Bias, whose individual and team accomplishments made him the program's most distinctive player. Bias was the only Terp to be named Player of the Year in the Atlantic Coast Conference twice. A 6-foot-8 forward, he led Maryland to its only ACC tournament championship since 1958 and increased the school scoring record with an astonishing blend of grace and power. Bias seemed to get bigger and better on the road, and the fact is that he had a so-so introduction to Cole Field House, where he ended his high school career.

The semifinals and championship games of the Maryland Public Secondary Schools Athletic Association tournament for boys were among the most enduring rituals at Cole. From 1956, the first March it was open, through 2002, three and then four state titles were decided each year at Cole. Tiny schools from western Maryland and the Eastern Shore would proudly bus in half their towns, but the best crowds came on Saturday night, when the largest schools decided the champion of what in 1989 changed from the AA classification to 4A.

Two years before a gimpy Willis Reed limped onto the floor and inspired his New York Knick teammates in game 7 of the NBA finals against the Los Angeles Lakers, Harold Fox did the same for North-western High of Prince George's County in the 1968 Class AA final. Leaving the floor with an injury in the second quarter, Fox came back and collected 21 points and 16 rebounds in a stirring win over Walt Whitman of Montgomery County. Buzzy Braman's reputation as a shooting guru began in 1972, when he led Springbrook past Bladensburg. In 1990, John Brady scored his lone state title in 12 trips to Cole, as an up-tempo philosophy helped his Annapolis Panthers beat High Point, 106-102, at a maddening pace for a high school game with eight-minute quarters.

Situated in Beltsville, a few miles from College Park, High Point won three state championships from 1982 to 1992, and the first was its most memorable. A step over half-court, Vernon Butler took an inbounds pass and launched a 40-footer at the regulation buzzer that beat Prince George's rival Northwestern and Bias, 54-52. Butler appeared to have stepped out of a time machine. He wore a flattop—Jim Kehoe would have loved his look—and he actually let his hair grow longer when he played for the U.S. Naval Academy, where his muscle helped David Robinson lead the Midshipmen to an NCAA tournament regional final in 1986.

In that 1982 state 4A final, Bias scored 18 points, more than a third of his team's total. With his 19, Butler did the same, and it was obvious who worked harder at basketball and had a better understanding of the game. Butler saw the ball, moved without it, and leaned on Bias all night. There were at least a half dozen other major college prospects on the Cole floor that night, but Bias's raw physical talent stood out. Beaten on defense, his fast-twitch fibers let him recover and block shots. Bias threw down spectacular dunks and had the makings of what would become an elegant jump shot. It included a hang time that defied gravity, and Lefty Driesell was drooling over him.

Maryland and North Carolina State went the hardest after Bias, who had warmed to the game late in his adolescence, then grew frustrated when big men like Butler attempted to rattle him with physical play. During one Northwestern game, Bias threw the ball at an official. In his final season at Maryland, he hurled one at an opponent from Notre Dame, but took umbrage when his behavior was mentioned. If all the fouls opponents laid on him were called, he objected, he wouldn't have to throw elbows.

Despite that incident, Bias charmed officials with a 1,000-watt smile and his physical superiority, as his demeanor developed along with his game. Bias had been cut by his junior high team, and when he came to College Park, there were no expectations that he would become one of the best players in the nation. He wasn't the Terps' most publicized underclassman, and not even their most prominent local. With Ernie Graham, Albert King, Greg Manning, and Buck Williams moving on, Driesell was in desperate need of some offense in 1981–82, and Adrian Branch was eager to provide it. The Terps were only 5-9 against ACC competition, but Branch delivered a freshman record of 15.2 points a game. A 6-8 left-hander with an assortment of shots and moves, Branch started every game as a rookie and quickly was given carte blanche at the offensive end. When an otherwise subpar Maryland team upset top-ranked Virginia and Ralph Sampson in overtime at Cole on February 27, 1982, an outcome that kept the Terps from falling off the ACC radar, they had 20 field goals. Twelve came from Branch, who got by Jeff Jones for the jump shot that beat the Cavaliers and gave him 29 of the Terps' 47 points.

Coming out of DeMatha Catholic High School in 1981, Branch had been a cocky, polished player who was a landmark recruit for Driesell. As coldly as Driesell was received at Dunbar High in Baltimore, his track record at DeMatha, which had the nation's most prominent prep program, wasn't much better. Dutch Morley had been the only player Maryland got out of DeMatha in the 1970s. Stags coach Morgan Wootten had graduated from Maryland with a physical education degree in 1955 and objects to any suggestion that he has ever stiffed his alma mater, which passed over him twice when it was looking for a coach. Terp fans felt jilted over the years as DeMatha players like Adrian Dantley, Danny Ferry, and Joseph Forte bypassed Maryland and became All-Americans. Wootten points to the 1960s, when he sent Gary Ward and Mickey Wiles to Maryland. Morley and Branch played for Driesell, Maryland was Steve Hood's first college team, and Jerrod Mustaf began his college career there. Duane Simpkins ran the point in the mid-1990s for Gary Williams, whose 2002 recruiting class included Travis Garrison.

"It amazes me when people say, 'How come you send all of your players to North Carolina?' They need to study my record," said Wootten, America's most successful high school basketball coach ever, with 1,271 wins over 45 seasons. "Far more of my players have gone to Maryland than people realize. I've had over 150 players get college basketball scholarships, and more of them have gone to Maryland than any other school. There are a lot of factors that go into that decision. A lot of kids want to spread their wings, and go away from home."

Turning out Olympic sprinters and NFL prospects, DeMatha has become an athletic power across the board, the Washington area's

Adrian Branch, attempting to drive around North Carolina's Matt Doherty, had a knack for creating his own shots, which allowed him to leave Maryland in 1985 as the program's No. 2 all-time scorer. (Maryland Sports Information.)

counterpart to Moeller High in Cincinnati and Mater Dei in Los Angeles. Basketball remains its signature sport, however, as the Stags attract some of the best young prospects in the Washington, D.C., area and even on the East Coast. DeMatha is located little more than a two-mile drive south on Route 1 from College Park, and it was a coup for Driesell when Branch committed to Maryland. Northwestern is even closer. Bias could walk from his high school gym to Cole in 20 minutes, but the nuances of the college game seemed light-years away. He started Maryland's 1982–83 opener, but after Penn State embarrassed the Terps in Baltimore, Bias began the next two games on the bench. His third start came in an encouraging double-overtime win over No. 3 UCLA on December 23, but Bias wasn't in the starting lineup for good until late February, when Maryland made a surprise run into the NCAA tournament at the end of a strange season.

The sophomore class included Driesell's son Chuck. He played 42 minutes all season, but was inserted at the end of a close game at North Carolina on January 12. With Branch covered, Chuck drove for a potential game-winning basket, which was swatted aside by Michael Jordan. A month later, the defending NCAA champions went down to a 106-94 defeat at Cole, as the second half saw Maryland score 68 points and Herman Veal trigger a devastating transition game and clamp down on Jordan.

That conquest came two weeks after the Redskins had beaten the Miami Dolphins in Super Bowl XVII, but sporting life inside the Beltway wasn't serene for long. A campus judiciary board disciplined Veal after finding him guilty of unwanted sexual advances toward a female student, and he was suspended for the remainder of the season. Driesell responded by contacting the victim and asking her to withdraw the charges. His power play included some tactless remarks to the media, including "I've got some clout around this campus, and we'll see how much I have" and "I don't care about the women's center. I'm the men's center."

As a storm raged around the program, Bias quietly picked up his game. He averaged a modest 7.1 points and 4.2 rebounds as a freshman, but his basket beat the buzzer and Tennessee-Chattanooga in the first round of the NCAA tournament. The Terps were eliminated in the second round by top-ranked Houston, which didn't lose in the tournament until everything went right for N.C. State in the championship game.

Bias remained tentative against savvier players who came close to matching his size and quickness. While Branch knew how to avoid the reach of defenders and find the space to get off his pretty jumper, Bias seemed to wade into double teams, even at the start of his junior year.

As the observer of officials for the Atlantic Coast Conference, Paul Baker sat on press row at Cole from 1981 to 1999, and he remembers a game when it all clicked for Bias.

"He had not been that highly recruited," Baker said. "Bias had been nasty and abusive at a summer camp, and instead of having college coaches come to him, he repelled them. He was still a diamond in the rough, and in his freshman year, he couldn't put the ball on the floor. You could see that he liked to shoot from the outside and that he didn't want to be a power forward. Even though he blossomed as a sophomore, he still seemed stifled and could use maybe one baby dribble before he shot or passed. That changed early in his junior year. When Maryland beat Ohio State, he was double-teamed on the foul line extended. He had a devil of a time getting rid of the ball, kept pivoting, not using his dribble. Finally, he broke through the double team, put the ball on the floor, took two giant steps, and dunked. Lefty jumped up off the bench, the two made eye contact, and after that he took off. It was an epiphany. Bias became a moving chess piece rather than a postage stamp."

Keith Gatlin's stock rose along with Bias's. A top point guard from Grimesland, North Carolina, Gatlin had turned down several Tobacco Road schools to come to Maryland, where he began the 1983–84 season as a freshman reserve. Bias was one of the first college players to perfect the reverse dunk, and dunk off lob passes. Usually they were thrown by Gatlin.

"When his sophomore season began, the light wasn't on in Lenny's head yet, but you could see that he was going to be a megastar," Gatlin said. "You could tell that he had the talent, that it was going to be his team and he was going to be the man. In the second half of the season, he did more than just take his game to another level. He went to another planet."

There was considerable buzz over the Terps in November 1983, as they were No. 8 in the preseason rankings. On Christmas Eve the Terps beat No. 6 Boston College and Williams, its second-year coach. A week and a half later Maryland played its ACC opener in Raleigh, and beat defending NCAA champion N.C. State. Bias was coming on, but Ben Coleman was the most productive player up front, and the team still bore Branch's stamp until late January, when Branch, then a junior, and seldom-used senior guard Steve Rivers were charged with possession of marijuana and suspended. Branch received probation before judgment and rejoined the team two weeks later. In his absence, the Terps dropped a pair of double-overtime games on the road, at Georgia Tech and Wake Forest. The skid continued when Duke won at Cole, but Gatlin made the

North Carolina's Brad Daugherty wasn't the only player beaten by Len Bias, who arrived at Maryland with raw potential and left as the Terps' only two-time ACC Player of the Year. (Maryland Sports Information.)

most of his expanded role and Bias became a constant. In a pivotal triple-overtime win at Clemson that ended the Terps' ACC losing streak at three games, Bias played the entire 55 minutes.

Maryland was loose when it went to the ACC tournament at the Greensboro Coliseum. The Terps were the second seed with a 9-5 record, and the weight of expectations was on North Carolina, which had gone unbeaten against conference competition. The Tar Heels' 14-0 mark included an easy win at Cole, where Jordan did a windmill dunk as Driesell and Dean Smith got a head start on the coaches' obligatory postgame handshake. Maryland got past N.C. State in the first round. In the semifinals, its balance beat Wake Forest and Duke took out North Carolina. The final changed complexion at the half. Johnny Dawkins was on fire in the first 20 minutes, but then Driesell went to a 2-3 zone that cooled off the Blue Devils' streak shooter, Coleman and Veal sealed off the inside, and Bias went berserk. The Terps outscored Duke 47-32 in the second half, as Bias finished with a career-high 26 points on 12-for-17 shooting, not that anyone could remember any of his misses. Absent from the top ten vote-getters on the all-ACC team, Bias was the unanimous tournament MVP.

Maryland coaches carry a different view of Southern hospitality, and for a half century they have echoed the same complaint: The Terps are outsiders in a conference that caters to its four members from North Carolina. Williams continues a lament that began when he was a player and the tournament was conducted every year at Reynolds Coliseum, on the campus of N.C. State. Bud Millikan had it the roughest of any Terp coach, in an era when television wasn't yet regulating the work of officials, but Driesell had suffered a heap of heartbreak on Tobacco Road. After his sixth ACC final in 15 seasons, he finally gloated over a tournament championship and vowed to attach the trophy to the hood of his car and drive around North Carolina.

The Terps didn't last long in the NCAA tournament, where Illinois beat them in the Mideast Regional semifinals at Rupp Arena in Lexington, Kentucky. Driesell became background noise as Georgetown played in its second national championship game in three years and beat Houston. The focus was on the post war between Patrick Ewing and Akeem Olajuwon, but the Hoyas' top scorers in the championship game were two players from Baltimore's Dunbar, Reggie Williams and David Wingate. There was little joy in the city, however, since Colts owner Bob Irsay had moved his NFL franchise to Indianapolis two days before the Final Four.

Bias and Branch combined to average 37.1 points in 1984–85, but both missed the dirty work that Coleman and Veal had performed under the basket. For three seasons, theirs had been an uneasy alliance, as author Lewis Cole wrote in his book about Bias, *Never Too Young to Die.* "As freshmen, [Jeff] Baxter and Bias both sat a lot," Cole wrote. "They would goof on the court antics of the players, making fun especially of Adrian Branch, the team's top scorer, a tricky forward whom they sometimes called Tragic Magic since he often failed in his attempts to imitate the famous feats of the nonpareil Magic Johnson."

Derrick Lewis, a lean 6-7 freshman from Archbishop Carroll in Washington, D.C., added his uncanny shot-blocking ability to the mix in 1984–85, but Bias topped the Terps with 6.8 rebounds a game, the lowest average ever for a Maryland leader in that category. A nondescript regular season included four straight losses in February, which delayed Driesell's 500th win. When it finally came, against Towson State on February 21, he rubbed it in during a 91-38 blowout. One more conference win would have given the Terps a share of the regular-season title in the ACC, where there was no clear power and one game separated the top five teams.

Bias became Maryland's second ACC Player of the Year, but the Terps could not repeat at the conference tournament, where they had a feeble 13-point loss to Duke in the quarterfinals. Fortunately for Driesell, the NCAA tournament had expanded to 64 teams, and Maryland was shipped off to Dayton, Ohio, for an eight-team subregional on the Ides of March that may never be matched for fascinating subplots and great finishes. The bill on March 15 saw Michigan, the top seed in the Southeast Regional, survive a four-point scare from Fairleigh Dickinson. Villanova staved off Dayton on its home court and won by two. Miami of Ohio and Ron Harper, who averaged 24.9 points, extended Maryland to overtime, and Driesell was not thrilled about his second-round match-up. Winless in the NCAA tournament since 1959, 13th-seeded Navy had routed Louisiana State, 78-55.

With Robinson and Butler, the Midshipmen were unafraid of the Terps, but Maryland held Navy at bay on St. Patrick's Day. The other second-round game at the Dayton Arena produced an upset, as Villanova slowed Michigan and picked up steam. At the Sweet 16 in Birmingham, Alabama, the fifth-seeded Terps became coach Rollie Massimino's third victim. Villanova followed with wins over North Carolina, Memphis State, and Georgetown as it beat two No. 1 seeds and two No. 2s en route to the most improbable championship in the history of the NCAA tournament.

Bias considered turning pro in 1985 and joining the early-entry candidates for the NBA draft that included Karl Malone, but Boston Celtics general manager Red Auerbach was in the crowd that advised him to return to Maryland for his senior season. With Branch's eligibility completed, the focus on Bias became even greater in 1985–86. The cover of the media guide showed him finishing a reverse dunk on Duke's David Henderson. The inside cover listed his accolades, and the first page bore a photo gallery of Bias at *Playboy* magazine's All-American "Team Weekend." Bias averaged 23.2 points, the most by an ACC player in a decade, but his leadership became a paradox during a stretch in which Maryland lost seven of eight games and slipped to 11-10 overall.

Driesell wanted to grab hold of a heckler one night, and Dave Dickerson, then a freshman and later assistant coach, took in all of the turmoil. "My freshman year, College Park was a lot like it was in 2001," Dickerson said. "Football was great, they were ranked No. 1 in the preseason. There was a lot of hype over basketball, but then we hit that rough stretch. I was too young to tell what was going on, but now I know that there was panic amongst the coaching staff."

Bias's body had been strengthened by a serious weight-training regimen, but his style included wearing an ermine-trimmed leather coat, and the duality of his nature was most apparent in that season's series with North Carolina. The Terps overcame their midseason slump and picked up speed on January 14, when Bias was suspended for breaking curfew amid rumors of more serious transgressions, including drug use. Bias returned and scored 41 points against Duke two weeks later, but it wasn't enough to avert a fifth straight loss and inquiries about Maryland's possibly being host to early games in the NIT. When Maryland went to Chapel Hill on February 20, the Tar Heels, conversely, were ranked No. 1 and were looking to add to their mastery of the Terps.

The previous year in Chapel Hill, Maryland had given Carmichael Auditorium a parting gift. The Terps had a three-point lead and possession with 23 seconds left, but then Branch and Gatlin missed free throws, and North Carolina escaped with a 75-74 victory. Now the Tar Heels were playing in a facility that was the most opulent in the ACC, and they were unbeaten at the Dean Smith Center. Maryland didn't play like a team headed to the NIT. Down by nine with two minutes left, the Terps rallied. Baxter sent it into overtime, and Gatlin scored when he in-bounded the ball off Kenny Smith's back, but the sequence that lingers in the minds of Maryland fans was supplied by Bias. He soared above the defense for a jump shot on the left wing, then swiped the ball from Kenny Smith and threw down a reverse dunk on Warren Martin. It was all instinct, made more amazing by the fact that Bias was out of position.

"Lefty wanted us to press, but Lenny forgot to defend the in-bounds pass and headed upcourt," Gatlin said. "When he finally remembered what he was supposed to do, he caught Kenny Smith turning to go up court. He was out of position, and that's why he caught Smith off guard. Being the first visitor to win at the Dean Dome, that was as good as Christmas morning. I'll never forget it."

Driesell had gone 2-14 at Carmichael, and now he was 1-0 at the Smith Center after a 35-point display by Bias. "If Leonard Bias ain't the player of the world," he said, "people don't know basketball."

That game iced Bias's second straight ACC Player of the Year Award, which added to his awkward relationship with a prying press. "Lenny was a terrific player but one of those kids who didn't like dealing with the media," said Don Markus, then the beat writer for the *Sun*. "He was still trying to figure us out. He would hide on us, and say, 'I want other people to get the credit.' All of us wanted to do a big story on him. The team still flew commercial then, and during a delay in Greensboro, Joe Blair got him for me. I told him, 'You're a pleasure to watch but a pain in the butt to cover.' In the interim, he announced he wasn't talking to the media the rest of the year. We ran a photo he liked; it showed a necklace that his mother had given him. At practice he asked if he could get a copy of the photo. He had just been named ACC Player of the Year, so I asked him for a comment. He said, 'You know I'm not talking to the media.'"

Baxter fueled another upset of North Carolina in the first round of the ACC tournament, but the Terps lost in the semifinals to Georgia Tech, and Bias's college career ended with a 70-64 loss to Nevada–Las Vegas in the second round of the NCAA tournament. Rebel coach Jerry Tarkanian said he thought Bias was the best player in the nation, and didn't dwell on how he ran defenders at Bias and dared him to put the ball on the floor. Len Bias finished his career with 2,149 points, an ACC championship, and a highlight reel that ran for hours, but everyone agreed that he was going to be even better as a pro.

13

THE TEAM BANQUET at the conclusion of every season is meant to be a celebration, a night to acknowledge recent achievements and show appreciation for career contributions. A succession of sporting greats had enlivened Maryland banquets in the 1970s, but in 1986 Len Elmore crashed the party with a blunt message that made the gathering of coaches, players, family, and boosters squirm.

After concluding his Terp career in 1974, Elmore had played in the NBA, entered Harvard Law School, and dabbled in commentary on National Public Radio, and he had never shied away from a controversial observation. Elmore had come to College Park in 1970, during an era of great unrest. Campuses had graduated from the keg parties depicted in *Animal House* to recreational drug use, and the movie's antihero, John Belushi, was dead from freebasing cocaine. Elmore had been in the NBA when its quality of play and status as a major league were threatened by an epidemic of substance abuse, which counted among its casualties John Lucas, another former Terp great. At Maryland, Elmore had played with Tom McMillen, a Rhodes scholar, and others who used college basketball as an avenue. Now he worried. In three of the past four seasons, a Terp veteran had been suspended for his behavior, first Herman Veal, then Adrian Branch and Len Bias. Was the current generation of Maryland players being used by basketball? Were they wasting a grand opportunity? Were they strong enough to avoid the possible pitfalls of being prominent basketball players?

"I just talked about guys doing destructive things instead of what they were supposed to do," Elmore said of his remarks at the 1986 basketball banquet. "I didn't name names, I just said that destructive behavior would limit your ability to reach your potential. I said, I've been through most everything you guys have been through. My generation had experienced some of the same mistakes associated with conduct. We didn't have anybody say, 'This is wrong, it's going to kill you or ruin your future.' We saw people navigate dangerous waters and have their ships sunk. My generation experienced the end of the civil rights movement, the beginning of feminism, the climax of the Vietnam War, so much upheaval in the world. We grew up in an era of redefined mores, with a lot of mixed messages. We heard one thing one day, something else the next. I was someone who was able to say that this is not the direction to take. If you're able to stop, stop. If you can't, get some help. To this day, I still talk about that.

"I would hope that Lefty [Driesell] knew me well enough to know that I was going to speak my mind. Coach got ticked off when I said what I said. I don't blame Lefty, but I think his recruiting had leveled off. There came a point where he didn't recruit the right kids, [he recruited] kids who didn't even comport with his picture of student-athletes. From the late 70s on, some—I'm not saying all—some of his recruits did not have the same character profile. Everything I said was said with deep affection for Coach. I wouldn't say anything to intentionally hurt Coach. He was like a second father to me, and remains so. I'm not sure how Coach took it. It was misinterpreted if anyone thought I had a malicious intent, but these issues were far too important to remain silent on."

Elmore's remarks about the dangers of fame were not taken well by some players. A few felt that, more than anyone, Elmore should have known what a seedy enterprise college athletics could be.

Sadly, Elmore turned out to be prophetic.

Len Bias had many awards to claim that night. He wasn't just Maryland's best senior or its best player. Bias was a first-team All-American, the only Terp to be named Atlantic Coast Conference Player of the Year twice. The local kid had made real good, and the Boston Celtics maneuvered to make him the cornerstone of their future, the prospect who would learn from, and then succeed, the great Larry Bird in Red Auerbach's master plan for NBA domination. On Memorial Day, Bias went to the Boston Garden to watch the Celtics begin their championship series against the Houston Rockets. Twenty days later, on June 17, 1986, America's best collegiate players gathered at Madison Square Garden's Felt Forum for the NBA draft.

North Carolina's Brad Daugherty was taken first, by Cleveland. Boston traded up to Seattle's second pick and took Bias, who told reporters that his first purchase was going to be a Mercedes-Benz. N.C. State's Chris Washburn, Auburn's Chuck Person, Kentucky's Kenny Walker, Memphis State's William Bedford, and Michigan's Roy Tarpley followed as the lottery picks. The first round included the most star-crossed collection of talent ever welcomed into the NBA, but none would fall as abruptly as Bias.

Bias joined his father and his agent for a short flight to Boston's Logan International Airport. The next day they met the New England media and representatives of the Reebok shoe company, as Celtics

Leaving Maryland as its all-time leading scorer in 1986, Len Bias was sitting on top of the world when he was the second player selected in the NBA draft. Less than 48 hours later, Bias died of a cocaine overdose. (Maryland Sports Information.)

officials patted themselves on the back for snatching up a youngster whose potential matched that of the exciting young guard in Chicago, Michael Jordan. After being feted in his new hometown, Bias returned to College Park exhausted but prepared to do some serious partying. He went for a postmidnight beer run with Brian Tribble, a friend, but alcohol was the tame aspect of the celebration that night on campus. It was not the first cocaine party at Washington Hall, but it would be the last for Bias.

The strong, impressive athlete who had been nicknamed "Horse" kept indulging until he went into convulsions and cardiac arrest. At 6:33 A.M., Tribble made an emergency 911 call. Bias was rushed to Leland Memorial Hospital in Hyattsville. Efforts to revive him were futile, and at 8:55 A.M. on June 19 he was pronounced dead. Less than 48 hours after Bias's basketball ability had provided him with lifetime financial security, that life was over, taken by a cocaine overdose.

The entire University of Maryland, not just Driesell and his basketball team, entered a crisis that might have been the biggest in its history, at least since the accreditation scare of the 1950s. Football programs that disregard the rules have been given the "death penalty," that is, been shut down by the NCAA, but no college team or university has experienced the relentless scrutiny, castigation, and introspection that Maryland endured after Bias's death. Cole Field House took on the mien of a funeral home. The Reverend Jesse Jackson was among the speakers at Bias's funeral. No congressman wanted to be viewed as soft on drugs, and Bias's death led to a flood of knee-jerk legislation on Capitol Hill requiring mandatory minimum jail sentences. Driesell wanted to remain as coach, but the ensuing scandal alleged a cover-up of the party that killed Bias and widespread indifference to the academic progress of his players.

Some were indicted by the state's attorney for Prince George's County. All were deemed guilty by association.

"It was one of the hardest times of my life," said Dave Dickerson, a Maryland assistant coach for Gary Williams who was a freshman when Bias was a senior. "It seemed like the world turned its back on us. The only thing we understood was each other, our teammates. I remember Lefty fighting for his livelihood and the university trying to protect its image. It was so hard on us, I can almost feel that despair just talking about it. I had guarded one of the best players in the nation in practice; I matched up with Lenny every day. For him to die like that, with a cocaine overdose and the media attention that it received, it was overwhelming. I couldn't handle it. A lot of us couldn't handle it. That night impacted a lot of people in a negative way. No one really came to our side. We were all made out to be bad students and drug addicts. The team and the program were in disarray."

Keith Gatlin had entered Maryland a year behind Bias, whose ability to finish would help Gatlin pile up 573 of his school-record 649 assists. A review of the players' academic performance found that Bias had stopped attending school, and Gatlin was among the players in academic trouble. He was not allowed to play in 1986–87, but Gatlin found the resolve to return to College Park. Eighteen months after Bias's death, he rejoined the team.

"You're sitting on a college campus, and the TV and newspapers are quoting anonymous sources who say that everyone on the team was involved in drugs and alcohol," Gatlin said. "I never drank or smoked. To this day, I'll never be remembered as a quality person or for setting Maryland's assist record. It's always, 'Oh, he played with Len Bias.' A lot of us were written off as bad kids. Lefty, he didn't have the time to give us the attention we needed. I totally went into a funk. My mom told me that if I didn't go back to Maryland, I would be part of the problem, so I gutted it out."

Driesell sweated through a long, hot summer in which the coaching profession portrayed him as a scapegoat, educators said he had to go, and politicians split over his future. Chancellor John Slaughter was a deliber-ate man, and he formed a task force to study the situation as a grand jury began to probe Bias's death. Slaughter and Driesell testified, and the state's most powerful figures, from Governor William Donald Schaefer on down, voiced opinions as the coach fought to hold on to his job. Baltimore Orioles owner Edward Bennett Williams, a lawyer whose clientele had included Senator Joseph McCarthy and Jimmy Hoffa, represented Driesell in court and buyout negotiations. Driesell was absolved by the grand jury, but Slaughter refused to give the coach the vote of confidence he had campaigned for. Driesell's contract called for him to be paid $150,000 per year well into the 1990s, and he would not leave without being pushed. On October 29, 1986, a little more than four months after Bias's death, Driesell announced his resignation at Cole Field House.

With a toll that included Owen Brown and Chris Patton, three of Driesell's Maryland players had died before they turned 24. In 2001, a week after his Georgia State team had lost to the Terps in the NCAA tournament and eight months before one of the Panthers' players was killed in an auto accident, Driesell was asked how he dealt with those deaths. "I really don't know how to answer that," Driesell said. "I'm a Christian myself. I'm a Presbyterian. We believe in predestination. The Lord has a time for all of us to go. You're going to go, it's already written. I'm going to go, it's already written. If you try to handle it any other way, you'd be in trouble. When somebody passes, you just have to figure it's the Lord's will."

Driesell shrugs off any questions about his place in the history of college basketball. He never intended to change the game, but he did, as

Keith Gatlin set Maryland's game, season, and career assists records by getting the ball to Len Bias, whose death cast a shadow over Gatlin and everyone associated with the Terps. (Maryland Sports Information.)

much as any man whose career was never validated by the Final Four. The NCAA expanded the recruiting section of its rule book and its tournament because of the kinds of excesses that Driesell luxuriated in. He taught a generation of coaches how to sell a program. Midnight Madness, the expansion of the NCAA tournament, the 35-second shot clock—all bear his influence. He coached in four NCAA regional finals and six ACC tournament championship games, and finished his 40th season in the business with 782 wins, a total surpassed only by Dean Smith, Adolph Rupp, Bob Knight, and Jim Phelan of Mount St. Mary's. Driesell's backers believe he should be in the Basketball Hall of Fame; detractors first talk of the death of Len Bias.

Coaches and some newspaper columnists argued that Driesell shouldn't have been blamed for Bias's overindulgence. Cynics countered that if Driesell had gotten his teams to fulfill their potential and gone to the Final Four, or won more than one ACC tournament, he might have been allowed to stay at Maryland, but his off-the-court record included too many black marks for Slaughter. Too few players had taken school seriously, and too many had faced criminal charges.

That wasn't enough to justify his removal, according to Robert Novak, the syndicated columnist and host of CNN's *Crossfire*, writing in the *Washington Post* on November 2, 1986. "No, Lefty is no saint," wrote Novak, who had become a Maryland fan because of Driesell. "In his desire to send a rested team onto the hostile courts of Tobacco Road, he sometimes brought his team on the road a day early, causing more classes to be missed. There are dark, unconfirmed reports from the 'task force' that in the case of three players, he actually interfered with their academic schedule so they could practice. In the sports world of 1986, those are not capital offenses. No big-time basketball coach is a saint, notwithstanding the canonization of Georgetown's John Thompson by the Washington media. Imagine what would have been Driesell's fate if he had enrolled a nonqualified student lacking even a high school diploma and used him to win a national championship in his only year as a student at the university. While Thompson was immune from criticism, Driesell would have been crucified on the sports pages of the *Washington Post* and *Baltimore Sun*."

Novak wrote that he would stay away from Maryland basketball for a while. Season-ticket sales fell 50 percent. Before Driesell was formally forced out, Slaughter chose to delay the start of practice two weeks and cancel the first semester's games. He wanted to give the Terps time to heal, but he also didn't know who was going to coach them. If the Lefty loyalists were angered when Slaughter said that Maryland basketball wasn't going to be business as usual, they were appalled when Driesell's successor was named.

Bob Wade's rise to power at Paul Laurence Dunbar High School in Baltimore coincided with Driesell's fall from grace in the state's largest city. The 41-year-old Wade was called "Flaky" by longtime friends, since his hands were supposed to be as soft as a snowflake. He had played several sports for Dunbar, then joined a Morgan State College football program that included Leroy Kelly and Willie Lanier, who would go on to be enshrined in the Pro Football Hall of Fame. Wade played four years in the NFL with the Redskins, Steelers, and Broncos, but an injury cut short his pro career. He had taught at a middle school in Howard County, then had become an assistant coach to Pete Pompey at Baltimore's Edmondson High.

Wade had taken over the storied basketball program at his high school alma mater in 1975 and rapidly grown from favorite son to father figure. At the time, Dunbar played second fiddle in Baltimore to Lake Clifton, where Ernie Graham led two Maryland Scholastic Association championship teams. Wade's first Dunbar team went 12-6. Graham transferred in, and the Poets went 23-1. Driesell, who already had Larry Gibson, recruited Dunbar's newest star. Graham left Maryland as its fourth-best all-time leading scorer, but before his exit the Baltimorean had charged that he had been slighted by Driesell. Mudslinging between the Dunbar and Maryland camps escalated in the early 1980s. Driesell said that Wade had been the first coach to tell him he would never get one of his players. Wade countered that Driesell had violated Dunbar procedure when he made a telephone call to the home of Reggie Williams, who happened to be the Poets' most-wanted recruit of the 1980s. Driesell said he would pay tuition for any of Wade's former players who wanted to finish their degrees, but added that the onus was on Graham to do the schoolwork.

Wade was the last man in Baltimore that a college coach wanted to anger. Driesell claimed that Wade shut him out of the entire city, but that was a moot point, because nearly every great player in Baltimore found his way to Dunbar. Prospects from the Madison Square Recreation Center went to Calvert Hall to play for coach Mark Amatucci. Everyone else seemed to land at Dunbar, where the basketball team was an important institution in the African American community. Wade's team was outfitted by Nike and showcased around the nation. It traveled to Las Vegas and Hawaii for tournaments against private and parochial schools with similar philosophies. The Poets offered those with a talent for basketball the best opportunity for higher education and the promise of NBA glory, and few coaches complained when players they had begun to develop transferred to Dunbar.

The import business at Dunbar began with Graham, and flourished in the early 1980s. From December 1981 to March 1984, Dunbar went 90-0 thanks to many players who had begun their high school careers elsewhere. David Wingate had started at Northern High, Tyrone "Muggsy" Bogues at Southern. Michael Brown had crossed town from Cardinal Gibbons. Wade and Dunbar won mythical national prep championships in 1983 and 1985. Bogues was replaced at the point by a transfer from McDonogh School, Taurence Chisholm. Kurk Lee came in from Calvert Hall and became the star guard. The Dozier twins, Terry and Perry, had helped Columbia's Hammond High become the first Howard County team ever to win a boys' state championship in 1983, then transferred to Dunbar. They repeated their junior years, as Dunbar officials explained that the quality of education in Howard County, which has a renowned school system, wasn't up to snuff with the curriculum in Baltimore City.

No matter where they had spent the ninth grade, the Poets came together and played some incredible basketball. After losing to them early in the 1982–83 season, DeMatha coach Morgan Wootten said it was the best high school team he had ever seen, and college recruiters camped in the gym at the corner of Orleans and Central. Assistant coaches like Georgetown's Craig Esherick and Kentucky's Leonard Hamilton became regulars, while Driesell visited in vain. Georgetown won an NCAA title in 1984 with a starting five that included sophomore Wingate and freshman Williams, the only Baltimorean to become a first-team consensus All-American in the 20th century. Conspiracy theorists in the Terrapin Club linked Dunbar to Georgetown's ascension past Maryland, and howled when it was learned that Hoya coach John Thompson was among the men who recommended Wade to Slaughter.

For the second time, Maryland had flirted with Wootten. The DeMatha coach had turned down a lucrative offer from North Carolina State in 1981, when the Wolfpack settled on Jim Valvano, and he wasn't keen on cleaning up the mess at his college alma mater. Dunbar had eclipsed DeMatha as a national prep power, but Wade admitted to being shocked when Slaughter offered him the job.

Maryland was desperate, and Slaughter did not make a safe choice. Wade had never worked in college athletics, and critics of the hire mentioned Gerry Faust, a high school football coach who had been a bust at Notre Dame. In addition to inheriting a tumultuous situation, Wade had to answer questions about being the first African American head coach in the ACC. Wade would come to lament that he wasn't "the people's choice." Compounding the difficulties facing Wade, Driesell's settlement called for him to remain in the athletic department. Lefty and his supporters in the Terrapin Club didn't trust Wade, and the sentiment was mutual.

"You can't do good in a program of this magnitude unless you have support," said Dickerson, who was entering his sophomore season when Wade was hired. "You have to have a couple of people in each area, the athletic department, the president's office, the booster club. Bob didn't have that. At the same time that he didn't cultivate the right people, the right people weren't there for him to cultivate. We felt everything he felt. Because he didn't get the support, we didn't get support. To put him in this situation was suicide. He lost his career because of the aftermath."

Wade couldn't construct a support system around him at Maryland. Slaughter, the chancellor who hired him, left College Park in 1988, the same week that Driesell found a new coaching job.

Misery mounted for Len Bias's parents in December 1990. Their son Jay, who had followed his big brother to Northwestern High, led it to a state championship, and tried to keep his career on track at Allegany Community College, was shot on a parking lot outside a mall jewelry store. He was pronounced dead at Leland Memorial Hospital, the same facility where his brother had been rushed in 1986.

The Celtics, the most storied franchise in the history of professional basketball, have not won an NBA championship since they drafted Bias.

14

BOB WADE WENT TO WORK at Maryland with a contract good for five years and fewer quality players than the school had had before, as the Terps of 1986–87 included five freshmen and four sophomores. The media guide, which featured more campus scenery than game action, tried to paint a rosy picture and offered this less-than-forthcoming description of the team: "Gone, for one reason or another, are seven members of last year's 19-14 Terp roster." Derrick Lewis was the lone returning starter, and John Johnson was the only other regular who had come back. Teyon McCoy and Steve Hood honored their commitments and came to Maryland, but Wade needed walk-ons to practice and picked up Tom Worstell off the lacrosse team.

The university was still reeling from the fallout of Bias's death, and it was an odd time around the capital Beltway. Moses Malone, the recruit who had gotten away in 1974, finally set up shop in Prince George's County, as he joined the Washington Bullets. Maryland's sinking athletic department continued to take on water, and football coach Bobby Ross walked off the job on December 2, 1986. Two days after Christmas, the Wade era began with a 76-58 victory over Winthrop, but the handcuffed Terps won just eight more games and went 0-14 in the Atlantic Coast Conference, their only winless season there.

The fan behavior of college students ranges from witty to tasteless, and Maryland's road reception included chants of "Just Say No," first lady Nancy Reagan's response to the drug dilemma. Some longtime Maryland backers wanted Wade to fail, but more enlightened boosters saw him lose to his former players, like Wake Forest's Tyrone Bogues and Clemson's Michael Brown, and could see that he had developed some outstanding talent at Dunbar. Rodney Monroe of St. Maria Goretti in Hagerstown was the state's top recruit from the high school class of 1987, and his interest in Maryland went from lukewarm to cold after Bias's death. Monroe headed to N.C. State, but Wade's initial recruiting class was a big hit.

There were complaints that Nike steered Alonzo Mourning away from Maryland and Georgia Tech and to Georgetown, but Wade's connections netted an initial recruiting class that featured Brian Williams of Santa Monica, California. Williams was flighty, but he was 6-10 and brought a wide array of skills across the country. After a year off to resolve academic issues, Tony Massenburg and Keith Gatlin returned, but Wade wasn't counting on the latter, as he had lined up another ball-handling guard.

Wade's power base in Baltimore extended to City Hall, where Mayor Clarence "Du" Burns, a onetime locker room attendant at Dunbar, had given hometown product Rudy Archer the key to the city. When Archer was at Southwestern High, he had given Wade's Poets fits, but he was an academic risk and spent two years with Bob Kirk at Allegany Community College in Cumberland. Wade successfully recruited Archer and got a solid season out of him, but it would come at a cost covered in irony.

Maryland improved from zero ACC wins to six in 1987–88. Lewis averaged 15.0 points and 7.6 rebounds, both team highs. Gatlin and Massenburg rejoined the team at the end of the first semester, and the Terps scored a huge win at Duke. Gatlin had been the goat in the 1986 ACC tournament, when his ill-advised inbounds pass frittered away what seemed to be a sure win over Georgia Tech. In the first round of the 1988 tournament, he shot Maryland past the Yellow Jackets, a victory that clinched an NCAA berth for the Terps. Kentucky eliminated Maryland in the second round, but a first-round victory over UC Santa Barbara was a landmark to savor. It was the Terps' only NCAA tournament victory between 1986 and 1994, but Wade's position unraveled just as he began to find his bearings on campus.

In the span of a few days in late March, the news broke that both Lefty Driesell and John Slaughter would leave Maryland. Slaughter, the university chancellor who had broken the color barrier among ACC coaches with his hiring of Wade, announced that he was taking the presidency of Occidental College in California. Driesell was going to be the new coach at James Madison University in Harrisonburg, Virginia.

Wade won the recruiting fight for Jerrod Mustaf, a 6-10 center, who, like Hood, was from DeMatha. Hood followed Driesell and transferred to James Madison, and Williams cited "philosophical differences" with Wade when he fled College Park for Arizona. Wade's critics ranged from talk show callers to State Senate President Mike Miller, and they got more ammunition in the off-season. McCoy, whose role had been reduced by the addition of Archer, announced that he would sit out the 1988–89 season, ostensibly to concentrate on his studies. He would have had a prominent role, since Archer became academically ineligible.

Gary Williams gave his alma mater the thumbs-up when he returned as Maryland's head coach in 1989, but his Terps were in for some glum seasons. (Maryland Sports Information.)

After a spike in Wade's second season, attendance at Cole dwindled again in 1988–89. Even diehard fans booed as the Terps returned to the ACC basement with a 1-13 record. Other than his wife, Carolyn, Wade had few backers, and he complained of working "under a microscope," as athletic director Lew Perkins did not quiet whispers that Wade wasn't running a clean ship. His third team won only as many games as his first, and that ninth victory in 1989 was strange. Mustaf ended the season on the bench with a knee injury, but Johnson scored 23 points as Maryland blew out regular-season champion N.C. State, 71-49, in the first round of the ACC tournament at the Omni in Atlanta. Wade collapsed afterward from dehydration and was hospitalized for what would have been his final game at Maryland, a 30-point loss to North Carolina in the semifinals.

Driesell's regime had been accused of not helping players in their pursuit of degrees, and Wade lost his job over looming NCAA violations, including one that he and his assistants had provided transportation from Baltimore to College Park for Archer as he attempted to regain his eligibility. In May 1989, Wade was forced to resign and was given severance pay of $120,000, as Maryland, awash in the red ink of an athletic department deficit that was now in the millions, continued to keep former coaches on its payroll. Bud Millikan had been 46 when Maryland pushed him out in 1967. Wade was only 44 when he fell off a coaching track that had become a tad too fast. His college record was 36-50.

On the surface, Wade's transgressions were laughable offenses in the looking-glass land of college athletics, but an NCAA investigation found more, as Gary Williams eventually learned.

As ill-prepared as Wade had been for an untenable situation at Maryland, Williams knew his way around the NCAA culture and college campuses, especially the one in College Park. He had found a place to play there in 1963, when the University of Pennsylvania said he wasn't Ivy League material. The young man from Collingswood, New Jersey, did not dispute that assessment; he was just enchanted with the idea of playing in the Palestra. Instead of spending his college career at that Philadelphia shrine, Williams found refuge in the biggest college basketball palace on the East Coast. Twenty-two years and eight jobs after he had concluded his playing career with the Terps, Williams returned to Cole Field House as head coach, and the program had come full circle.

Maryland had been a loser when Williams concluded his playing career, and it was a loser when he became head coach in 1989. Williams didn't mind being the underdog. In fact, he relished the part.

Before he got the Terps to their first Final Four in 2001, Williams was stung by a series of NCAA tournament upsets that ended Maryland seasons in the mid- and late 1990s, losses that led to the charge that he didn't know how to coach from the front of the pack. All he had known as a player and college coach was chasing programs with better players, resources, and traditions. Williams heard the catcalls that his Terps could have played harder in losses to Santa Clara in 1996 or Charleston in 1997 or St. John's in 1999. He told critics to chew on this: He was the first coach in the history of the NCAA tournament to take three teams that were seeded ninth or worse into the second round.

Wherever Williams had gone as a college coach, championships had followed; unfortunately, they were won by rivals. He worked for Boston College during the heyday of the Big East Conference, as Georgetown and Patrick Ewing cut a wide swath in 1984 and Villanova showed off that league's depth with its incredible run in 1985. Williams moved on to Ohio State, and Indiana and Michigan promptly won NCAA titles in 1987 and 1989, respectively. When he came to Maryland in 1989, the Atlantic Coast Conference's bark was worse than its bite, as the ACC had won just four NCAA titles in 35 seasons. Once Williams settled in at Maryland and the rebuilding job became harder than he had ever envisioned, that struggle was compounded by three straight titles for conference foes, as Duke won it all in 1991 and 1992, and North Carolina did in 1993.

Williams countered bigger and better talent in the early 1990s with a running, pressing style designed to mask Maryland's shortcomings. Before he had coached at Maryland or Ohio State or Boston College or even American University, that philosophy had taken hold with one of his first teams. Woodrow Wilson High in Camden, New Jersey, was undersized in Williams's first two seasons on the coaching staff there, and it didn't stop running when he took over the varsity in 1970–71. The result was a 27-0 record, a state championship, and an affinity for a frenetic style. As a player, Williams had itched for a faster pace. Millikan recruited him with the promise that Maryland was going to run, but Williams became a walk-the-ball-up point guard and directed teams that lost in the first round of the ACC tournament when he was a junior and senior.

"You look at him as a coach, you see him as a player," Millikan said in 2001. "He was every bit as intense as he is now, as hard-working a kid as you could ever imagine. A guy you would have to accept some in practice, because he would overdo it. He wasn't going to fight or punch somebody in the mouth, but if you tell him to cover somebody, he's going to crawl all over them. If he made an error in practice or a game, he would walk over to apologize to you, 'Coach, I shouldn't have taken that shot,' or 'Coach, I shouldn't have let that guy get by me.' He was the kind of kid you like to have."

Williams had craved Millikan's approval. He had little going for him other than basketball, and the losing affected Williams nearly as much as it did his coach. When he played for Maryland in the mid-1960s, the Terps became just another dysfunctional family to Williams. When he was 14, his father had abruptly said he wasn't coming home that night. His parents' marriage was in a shambles, and his mother moved to California. Williams's father never saw him play at Maryland, and for decades the two had a strained relationship. The son sought solace in basketball, his studies, and whatever work he could find. While his teammates joined fraternities and dreamed of bright futures, Williams went back to New Jersey each summer to see his high school sweetheart, Diane McMillen, and work menial jobs.

"I probably would have joined a fraternity if I had the money," Williams said. "Whatever I made in the summer was what I had to spend during the school year. I worked for RCA in Camden, ran an elevator there one year. Worked in a paper mill in Gloucester, Rubberoid. That was in the paper processing plant, in the oiler, where it was 100 degrees and you used to have to grease the machines. I collected trash in Collingswood one summer. That was a good job, because when you finished your route, you were done for the day. You got a couple of young guys and hustled, you could be out by 12 and still get paid for eight hours. Anything outdoors was great."

Anything in sports was greater. Williams completed his Maryland degree requirements during the 1967–68 school year and spent the next one assisting Tom Davis with the Terrapin freshman team. When he returned to New Jersey to teach in high school, Williams never thought he would return to College Park. He had just married Diane, and he didn't have that many happy memories of Maryland anyway.

After three years of high school teaching and coaching, Williams accepted an invitation from Davis to join him at Lafayette College in Easton, Pennsylvania. There wasn't enough money in the budget for Williams to work full time as an assistant basketball coach, so he also had to run the soccer team. Most coaches are control freaks, and no game is harder for them to watch develop than soccer. There are no timeouts, and substitution opportunities were severely limited in the 1970s, when Williams found himself arguing with officials over rules he wasn't clear about himself.

After following Davis to Boston College, Williams accepted an opening at American University in Washington, D.C., in 1978. At age 33, Williams walked into a situation that provided a baseline against which to measure Maryland's travail in the 1990s. Williams would be able to deal with sanctions and condemnation at Maryland because American was not exactly a free ride.

Chris Knoche, who joined play-by-play man Johnny Holliday as Maryland's radio analyst in 1999, had been Williams's first recruit at American. A native of Fairfax, Virginia, who would coach the Eagles from 1990 to 1997, Knoche had played at W. T. Woodson High and briefly at the University of Colorado. Williams added him to American when the Eagles' roster was as much in flux as the rest of the world. American did not have an on-campus arena, and home games were played at Fort Myer, in Arlington, Virginia. In Williams's second season, the nation followed the Iran hostage crisis, which figured heavily in Ronald Reagan's landslide victory over incumbent Jimmy Carter in the 1980 presidential election. Williams had read Sun Tzu's *The Art of War,* and his combativeness was heightened by coaching games on a military base.

"Gary is notorious for getting to the arena two and a half hours before tip-off," Knoche said. "He got that from *The Art of War.* The first one to the battlefield wins. It was particularly maddening to him, because a 15-minute ride from American to Fort Myer very quickly disintegrated into 40 during D.C. rush hour. Depending upon the climate, there were all kinds of security issues to deal with. A bunch of students would want to get to games early, park, and party. They wouldn't be on the lot 30 seconds before they were swarmed by security. One night, West Chester had the winning basket over-ruled, and their coach, Earl Voss, went ballistic. AU dressed in a weight room, and the facilities for the visitors were worse. Voss was screaming at the top of his lungs, prying things off the wall. He was finally subdued by MPs."

The Eagles practiced on campus, in a tiny gym with plywood nailed to the walls, but it was a desirable practice facility because Williams could close the doors and cajole his players without any female students or professors complaining about his language. Knoche and several other transfers laid the foundation for American teams that reached the National Invitation Tournament in 1981 and 1982, as the latter team prospered despite a devastating knee injury to forward Boo Bowers, one of the most gifted players Williams has ever coached.

American had never been to the NIT, and Williams used that success as a springboard to return to Boston College, which needed to replace Davis after he used an Elite Eight appearance to land the Stanford job. The Celtics were a force and college basketball was just as vibrant in Boston, as Jim Calhoun was putting Northeastern University on the map and Mike Jarvis would give Boston University some up seasons. Williams had developed a fondness for players who could ad lib their way to wins, clutch performers he called "unpredictables," guys like little Michael Adams, who gunned BC into the Sweet 16 in 1983 and 1985.

Williams spent four seasons at Boston College, and in 1986 he jumped to Ohio State. His first Buckeye team beat then–No. 1 Iowa, which was coached by Davis, one of his mentors, and played in the NCAA tournament. Williams leaned on another undersized guard, Jay Burson, compiled a 59-41 record, and put together some impressive recruiting classes that would get the Buckeyes a No. 1 seed in the 1991 NCAA tournament, but all was not rosy in Columbus.

Williams landed the state's top prospect, Jim Jackson, but he worried about the talent in the athletic department. Rick Bay, the Ohio State athletic director who had hired Williams, resigned in protest over the firing of Buckeye football coach Earle Bruce. Williams clashed with Jim Jones, Bay's successor, and weighed interest from Kansas and the Charlotte Hornets. Every road game is a guilt trip for coaches, and Williams's marriage to Diane was dissolving. After Wade was forced out at Maryland, the names of DeMatha coach Morgan Wootten, former Terp assistant George Raveling, UNC Charlotte's Jeff Mullins, and Southern's Ben Jobe were among those floated, but Maryland wanted Williams. Changing jobs for the third time in eight years, he accepted Perkins's invitation to clean up the three-year-old mess at his alma mater.

"It was screwed up when I was there as a student, and now it's screwed up again," Williams said of College Park in 1989. "This crap's got to stop. I had always had that dream, of this being a great university, and basketball being a very important part of why it's great."

It would be a dream deferred. In December 2001, Williams told *USA Today*'s Jill Lieber that his sideline behavior that bordered on the abusive stemmed from the anger he felt over the chilly relationship he'd had with his parents. His divorce was finalized in 1990, and he would become more remote in College Park. If Williams had a chip on one shoulder over his childhood, the NCAA was about to make him a well-balanced person by giving him a second chip to carry on the other shoulder.

15

GARY WILLIAMS LEFT an Ohio State tradition that included the 1960 NCAA championship. He thought he was going to run the basketball program at his alma mater, but instead he got a penal colony.

Williams was 44 when he returned to College Park. He longed to revisit his roots and settle down, but knew he would have to withstand an early storm. Maryland was being investigated for possible NCAA rules violations during the Bob Wade regime, but Williams had been assured that they were minor and that any possible penalties wouldn't hinder his quest to return the Terps to prominence.

Williams did not hit the ground around Route 1 running. Michael Tate, a highly regarded Wade recruit from Oxon Hill, rescinded his commitment to attend Maryland, went to Georgetown, and eventually played for Lefty Driesell at James Madison. The freshman class that entered in the fall of 1989 included Evers Burns and Kevin McLinton, and many thought both would have been better off playing college football. The returning players were coming off of Maryland's first 20-loss season since 1941, and the Terps' stock dipped just as that of college basketball spiked elsewhere in the state.

Navy had passed its prime once David Robinson left Annapolis, but in 1989–90 Towson State and Coppin State had veteran teams that would give Baltimore its first participation in the NCAA Division I tournament. Maryland dropped its third game under Williams, to South Carolina in a tournament in Richmond, Virginia. Three days later, the Terps lost to Connecticut, and they failed to heed Williams's warnings that Coppin State was not just another cupcake from the Mid-Eastern Athletic Conference, one of the two Division I leagues composed of historically black institutions. The Eagles had a fundamentally perfect post man in Larry Stewart, and other strong players from the Philadelphia area. They were hardened by Ron "Fang" Mitchell, who was among the older men from the neighborhood who had played pick-up at Woodrow Wilson High when Williams guided that Camden school to a New Jersey state championship.

Williams saw it coming, but after Coppin State handled Maryland, 70-63, on December 12, 1989, his players and a small crowd in drafty

Cole were in disbelief. So was the clerk at a drive-through liquor store in Baltimore, when the Eagle players told him what they were celebrating. It was Maryland's last nonconference loss at Cole, where it won its final 85 games against opponents outside the ACC.

The Terps regrouped after that wake-up call. Senior Tony Massenburg and two sophomores who had prepped in Prince George's County, Jerrod Mustaf and Walt Williams, made for a decent nucleus, and Maryland mustered six ACC wins. Two came over North Carolina, which got to the Sweet 16, but the Terps entered the conference tournament in Charlotte as the seventh seed and lost by 20 points to eventual NCAA tournament runner-up Duke.

That loss wasn't the worst that happened to Williams and the Terps that March. The results of the NCAA investigation were released. In addition to finding that Wade and members of his staff had provided transportation to class for Rudy Archer, the NCAA had found that recruits had been given clothing and players had sold complimentary tickets, a perk that had been winked at for decades around the nation. Administrators in College Park anticipated a slap on the wrist from the NCAA, but it had also found that Maryland had lacked "institutional control," and it came down hard. The Terps were banned from the NCAA tournament for two years. In addition, in 1990–91 they were not allowed into the ACC tour-

Walt Williams matured during his four seasons at Maryland. He had come from nearby Crossland High, and he surprised many when he stayed in College Park while other talented players fled the Terps' beleaguered program. (Maryland Sports Information.)

nament and could not appear on television, which begged an extension of the existential question: If a tree falls in the woods and there is no one to hear it, does it make a sound? If a college basketball team doesn't play on TV, does it exist?

Williams was livid. Recruits risked derision by committing to Maryland, and he second-guessed his decision to leave Ohio State. As booster support and box office receipts dropped in the aftermath of the death of Bias, Maryland had slashed its funding for nonrevenue sports like baseball and track and field but still hemorrhaged millions of dollars. The administration did not secure the high-priced legal counsel that most large athletic departments retain when scrutinized by the NCAA. When questioned by NCAA investigators, Williams resented any suggestion that he should be held responsible for the transgressions of his predecessor.

"I would have liked to coach my first team without distractions," Williams said of the 1989–90 school year. "During the day, my guys were getting questioned by the NCAA. I was meeting with lawyers from the NCAA, to ensure that now we were doing the right things. My point was, did I ever do a wrong thing before I came here? What do you mean, am I doing the right thing? That's an insult to my integrity."

Did Williams let NCAA investigators know he resented their line of questioning? "Yes," he said, "and they didn't like the fact that I was upset. I respect the college game as much as anybody. I can sleep at night. I don't set myself up as a saint, but I know what I've done as a basketball coach. I put too much into this game, and it's been my life. To have someone come in and tell me what I have to do to make sure I was running a program correctly. . . . Don't tell me how to run a program. I can tell you how to run a program. That's what upset me, the insinuation that because they had screwed up before, that was going to continue. It was kicking Maryland because they were down."

A decade later, his combustible nature was still evident. After Maryland lost a tough game at Temple in 2000, a young reporter pressed Williams at a podium with a line of questioning that might have been more effectively pursued in the hall two minutes later. With minicams rolling and the live feed going to some cable networks in New Jersey, Williams said "You're an idiot" three times. It was three months after his daughter Kristin and son-in-law Geoff had blessed Williams with his grandson David, an event that had been supposed to make him stop and smell the roses. Ten years earlier, when the NCAA tried to emasculate his program, Williams's pugnacity was at its peak, and he was notorious for clashes with security guards, fans, and anyone who stood between him and victory.

Williams's close friends in the coaching business call him "Wacko." If Lefty Driesell, with his Southern drawl and a penchant for dropping "I don't know, you know" into the response to any question that wasn't a softball, had come across like "Foghorn Leghorn," Williams was compared to another Warner Brothers cartoon character. In games and practices, when things didn't go just right, Williams would whirl and burst into paroxysms of profanity that brought the "Tasmanian Devil" to mind. In John Feinstein's book *A Season Inside: One Year in College Basketball,* Texas coach Rick Barnes said he didn't know how to swear effectively until he spent a season with Williams at Ohio State. When Williams directed his anger away from his players on the court and toward the men seated closest to him, his bench became a loud, profane place.

Billy Hahn, recruited by Driesell in 1972, had spent his Maryland career as a reserve and then went into coaching. Fired by Ohio University in 1989, when he admitted that he was "too young and stupid" to comprehend all the angles of being a head coach, Hahn had been in the job market when Williams came to Maryland. Desperate for work and grateful for a chance, Hahn partnered with Williams for 12 seasons, and sometimes wondered if it was worth it. After the 2001 Final Four helped him land the head coaching position at La Salle University, Hahn understood if the only image most Maryland fans had of him was as the guy who bore the brunt of Williams's bench bombast.

"I can understand if that's what they see," Hahn said. "I had people ask me, 'How can you put up with that? How can you have somebody yell at you like that?' They don't know Gary Williams like I know Gary Williams. Gary Williams wasn't yelling at me because it was Billy Hahn and he was mad at Billy Hahn. He was in a battle. There were a few times when I felt, 'I don't want to hear it, I'm an adult, enough already,' but as soon as the game is over, he never carries that with him. He demands . . . perfection is not the right word, he just demands that players do their best all the time. When something goes wrong on the court, you realize that he's going to vent his frustration at the people on the bench, because he doesn't want to yell at the people playing the game. He's going to vent, scream, curse, and yell. That was his style. Once you realize that, you learn to live with it. I knew what I was in for. It took a lot of energy to build Maryland back up, because the place was in a shambles. Look, maybe the biggest thing I learned from Gary Williams, he fought to get things done for the basketball program."

There were many battles to fight, and some wounds were self-inflicted. In May 1990, Williams was arrested and charged with drunken

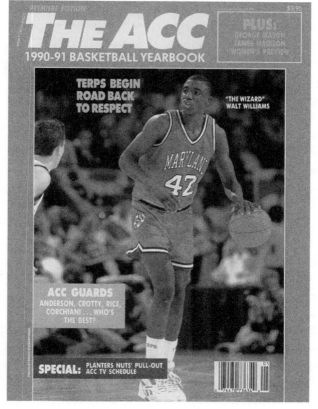

The star power of Walt Williams kept some of the region's top high school talent interested in the Terps at a time when Maryland didn't have much else going for it. (Maryland Sports Information.)

driving, and he received a fine and a year of unsupervised probation. Lew Perkins moved on to the University of Connecticut, and Andy Geiger took over as athletic director in October 1990 with the mandate to improve the academic performance of Maryland athletes. When Williams admitted that his staff had violated NCAA rules by watching pick-up games in the auxiliary gym at Cole prior to the previous season, the start of practice in October 1990 was delayed five days. There was a running battle over academic standards, as Maryland refused early admittance to recruits who eventually met the NCAA standards for freshman eligibility. Donyell Marshall of Reading, Pennsylvania, went to Connecticut and was consensus All-American in 1994, along with Jason Kidd, Grant Hill, Glenn Robinson, and Clifford Rozier. Lawrence Moten left Archbishop Carroll High in Washington and had a fine career at Syracuse. Williams wanted both and may have landed neither, but he felt as if he was recruiting with two sets of handcuffs, one applied by the NCAA and the other by Maryland, and wondered if he had committed professional suicide.

"I had moved around a lot," Williams said. "I spent four years at American, made a natural move to BC, and spent four years there. There were questions about my short stays when I went to Ohio State. Now I'm at my school, and nobody made me come here. I thought about it a lot. I told myself, 'Look, you took this job, you decided to come, you get it done.' I made up my mind to stay. I got stubborn."

Others took the NCAA probation as an opportunity to get out of town. Mustaf entered the 1990 NBA draft and was selected with the 17th pick by the New York Knicks. Teyon McCoy, who could not handle the rough riding of Williams, transferred to Texas. Other players who weren't capable of making as much of a contribution also left, and Williams fretted most of the summer whether Walt Williams would stay in College Park. Walt might not have been ready for the NBA, but other colleges implored him to transfer. Georgia Tech, fresh off its only Final Four appearance; St. John's, and others made serious sales pitches. They offered TV exposure and postseason play. Gary Williams didn't have much to offer, other than the chance to run the point with talent that was major conference in name only.

"Walt picked Maryland because he thought we could go to the NCAA tournament and play on television," Gary Williams said. "He said that he needed the attention if he expected to play after college. We didn't go to the NCAA tournament in his sophomore year, and we weren't going to be able to go in his junior and senior year. I thought we were going to lose him, but Walt was going to get to be able to play point guard for us, because we weren't going to be able to recruit a great one. At 6-8, he was going to get the experience of handling the ball. I said I would do everything I could to promote him, to get him the attention he deserves. If he doesn't stay, we stink."

College Park sits in Prince George's County, which dominated the state 4A high school championship in the 1980s, and Walt had been one of the county's best. He had made Crossland High a perennial at Cole each March. Walt led the Cavaliers to a state title in 1986. When he was a junior, Crossland lost the title game to Northwestern and Jay Bias. Springbrook and McLinton finally stopped the Cavaliers when he was a senior. That three-year run helped Crossland coach Earl Hawkins jump to the University of Maryland Baltimore County. As he pondered his options in the summer of 1990, Walt sought Hawkins's counsel and considered the health of his father, Walter Williams Sr.

"Maryland players were eligible to play immediately if they transferred to another school in 1990, and big-time schools were calling me to lean on Walt," said Hawkins, whose 31 rebounds for Gwynn Park in the 1970 state high school 1A tournament are believed to be the Cole record. "Walt Williams was not only the most talented player I ever had at Crossland, he was probably the most unselfish. He loved giving the ball up as much as scoring, one of those kids who loved to throw the lob for a dunk as much as be on the receiving end. Maryland and North Carolina are the only schools he visited when he was a senior. His parents always taught Walt the value of right and wrong. Loyalty, trust, the things that count with a person of substance, they were instilled in Walt."

Of course, Walt stayed, and won admirers beyond College Park as he carried Maryland over the next two seasons. Three days after North Carolina gave Dean Smith his 700th coaching victory with a 105-73 pounding of the Terps in Chapel Hill, Williams fractured the fibula in his left leg against Duke on January 12, 1991, proof of the adage that no good deed goes unpunished. The injury didn't end Walt's junior season, as he made a dramatic return six weeks later against Wake Forest and collected 21 points and eight rebounds in the regular season finale, a 78-74 overtime win at No. 25 Virginia. With Maryland banned from the ACC tournament for the only time, the Terps approached that game as if it were their postseason, and the victory in Charlottesville was cathartic.

Walt weighed his NBA chances but came back to College Park for one last uphill season. The effects of the NCAA sanctions had taken a toll on recruiting, and the 1991–92 roster included walk-ons like Glen Burnie's Mike Thibeault and DeMatha's Kurtis Shultz. The center was Chris Kerwin, a transfer from Old Dominion. Football lineman Lubo Zizakovic got in one game. Williams showed the way in just about every one, as his 26.8 points a game set a Maryland record and the ACC learned why Wade had nicknamed Walt "the Wizard."

The burden of carrying a team weighed on Walt for half his senior season. When defending NCAA champion Duke came to Cole on January 8, 1992, he scored 25 points but had 11 turnovers and no assists. He was then fitted for contact lenses, and went on the hottest roll ever experienced by a Terp. Williams scored at least 30 points in seven straight games, one shy of the ACC record that Wake Forest's Len Chappell had set in the early 1960s. During his streak, Walt made more than 60 percent of his shots and better than 55 percent of his three-pointers. Florida State had a Sweet 16 team that featured some fine perimeter talent, like Sam Cassell, Bob Sura, and Heisman Trophy winner Charlie Ward. All watched Williams destroy them in Tallahassee, and his tip-in with 1.3 seconds left beat No. 10 North Carolina in his next-to-last appearance at Cole.

"Walt once said that the basket looked like an ocean," McLinton said. "Everyone planned their defense to stop him. Teams knew he was going to shoot, and they still couldn't stop him. He made us all better players. I thought Walt should have been MVP in the ACC. Obviously, Christian Laettner was pretty good for Duke, but we wouldn't have been able to survive without Walt Williams."

Williams's influence extended beyond the court. Michigan's "Fab Five" had spread the popularity of Michael Jordan's baggy shorts, but throughout the Mid-Atlantic region young players wanted to be like Walt and pulled their socks high. In Norfolk, Virginia, the skinny center at Maury High named Joe Smith took to wearing longer socks.

Closer to home, Walt Williams let all the top young talent in the Washington area know that it was cool to play for Maryland. The DeMatha–Power Memorial game that featured Lew Alcindor in 1965 had been the most famous high school game ever at Cole, but the most hotly contested came in 1991. The city title game to decide bragging rights matched DeMatha against Dunbar. The Catholic power had a deft little point guard named Duane Simpkins. Dunbar, the Washington public schools champion, had its own lefty shooter, Johnny Rhodes. DeMatha won with a furious rally, as Simpkins and Rhodes were the game's MVPs. When Walt Williams was a senior, Rhodes, Simpkins, Exree Hipp of Harker Prep, and Stacy Robinson of DuVal all committed to play for Maryland, and Mario Lucas came in from Memphis, Tennessee.

That landmark class lost some of its depth when Robinson couldn't meet the NCAA standards for freshman eligibility. Even without him, that group of recruits gave Gary Williams the kind of foundation that Mike Krzyzewski had laid at Duke in 1982, when he brought in Mark Alarie, Jay Bilas, Johnny Dawkins, and David Henderson.

"Me and X [Hipp] had played AAU ball together, and we all looked up to Walt," Simpkins said. "My whole senior year of high school, just about every day after practice at DeMatha, I would go hang out with Walt. It got to the point where my father pulled me aside and reminded me that I was still in high school, but Walt and the rest of the guys were just cool to be around. We were all interested in Maryland, but Walt was the icing on the cake. He found it within himself to stick it out at Maryland when things weren't good. He could have gone anywhere, but he grew up on the same thing we did. We loved playing at Cole. It was a second home to some of us."

Walt Williams was the seventh pick in the 1992 NBA draft, and started his pro career with the Sacramento Kings. Before his rookie season was complete, he endowed the University of Maryland with $125,000, and the college should permanently recognize his contributions. Outside the home of the Baltimore Orioles stands a statue of Babe Ruth, who grew up a few blocks to the north. Michael Jordan is immortalized in a sculpture outside the United Center, where the Bulls fell off the NBA map once he left Chicago. On the promenade to the Comcast Center, Maryland should erect a monument to Walt Williams.

16

NO PLAYER MADE as big an impression at Maryland in two seasons as Joe Smith. When he came to College Park, the Terps were mired in a rut of eight straight losing seasons against Atlantic Coast Conference competition. When Smith was a sophomore, Maryland shared the ACC regular-season championship, and his role at the center of that turn-around made him the National Player of the Year in 1994–95. Three months later, the Golden State Warriors made Smith the No. 1 selection in the NBA draft, but despite Smith's accomplishments and acclaim, Gary Williams didn't think he was the most important catch in the recruiting class that arrived in 1993. "Keith Booth," Williams said, "was the one guy who legitimized our program."

Booth ended a long chill between the university's most prominent team and the state's premier public high school program, where he starred during its last high-water mark. Early in each of three decades, the 1970s, 1980s, and 1990s, Dunbar High in East Baltimore put together a team that was as good as any in the nation. The first group in that cycle put the largest city in Maryland on the prep basketball map. Each of the next two produced a mythical national champion, but that cycle didn't continue, due to a move that boosted most of Baltimore's public school sports teams, but diminished opportunity for the Poets and other boys' basketball teams to be major players in the prep game.

In 1992 the city joined the Maryland Public Secondary Schools Athletic Association, which had long conducted state championships for public schools in 23 counties. The chief beneficiaries of the move were the girls, whose seasons had rarely extended beyond city competition. Two Baltimore institutions that encompassed three schools and two sports stood to lose the most. The first was the City-Poly football rivalry, a Thanksgiving Day staple that was moved up in the calendar in order for the Knights and Engineers to participate in the state tournament that culminated at Byrd Stadium. The second was Dunbar basketball.

The Poets' debut in the state tournament at Cole Field House produced a team scoring record, as Booth scored 26 points to pace a 122-58 rout of Fallston in a Class 1A semifinal mismatch. A day later, Dunbar

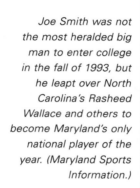

Joe Smith was not the most heralded big man to enter college in the fall of 1993, but he leapt over North Carolina's Rasheed Wallace and others to become Maryland's only national player of the year. (Maryland Sports Information.)

became the first Baltimore team to win a state title. The Poets began their membership in the MPSSAA with four straight championships and collected crowns in seven of their first nine. The only comparable run in tournament history had come from Allegany in the 1930s, when Cumberland schools apparently were the only members taking the sport seriously. Dunbar should have been proud of its dominance at Cole, but it only made the older ones among the "Poet Followers" wistful. They remembered when their basketball team had been *really* good, when it didn't have to deal with the travel and scheduling restrictions of the MPSSAA.

For decades, most African American boys in Baltimore who dribbled basketballs dreamed of playing for Dunbar. The program's first national exposure had come on Baltimore Street in 1973, when Dunbar beat DeMatha before a raucous crowd at the Civic Center. The Stags had Adrian Dantley and Kenny Carr, but the Poets of coach William "Sugar" Cain ran wild with Skip Wise on the wing and Larry Gibson in the paint. No longer did college recruiters drive directly from Washington, D.C., to Philadelphia in their search for talent, and no one appreciated the meaning of that 1973 game more than DeMatha coach Morgan Wootten. "That win did for Baltimore," Wootten said, "what the DeMatha-Power Memorial game in 1965 did for high school basketball nationally. It made everyone sit up and take notice."

A decade later, Dunbar earned a mythical national championship with the Bob Wade powerhouse that included Muggsy Bogues, Reggie Williams, and Reggie Lewis. The last of Dunbar's distinctive teams had played in 1992, when coach Pete Pompey had another perfect national championship team that featured three players. Michael Lloyd would star in the Big East Conference before academic questions ended his career at Syracuse. Donta Bright, a do-it-all player who seamlessly moved from the low post to the wing, would help the University of Massachusetts to its greatest basketball achievement, the 1996 Final Four. Like Lloyd, Bright was academically ineligible to play in the NCAA as a freshman. A year behind at Dunbar, Booth was determined to avoid the pitfalls that had slowed his older teammates.

Bright had introduced Booth, his first cousin, to basketball. Besides blood, they shared an affinity to mix it up under the basket. Booth was quick enough to guard anyone on the floor, but he most enjoyed the challenge of checking bigger players. Pompey allowed him to play the point occasionally, and while Booth lacked range on his jump shot, he spent sufficient time on his schoolwork and met the NCAA standards for freshman eligibility. Williams wanted Booth. He was a total package, and he was from Baltimore, where Terp basketball had become poison after a series of slights, whether real or perceived.

At the end of Ernie Graham's career, the *News American* had run a story in which he was critical of Lefty Driesell. It appeared just as Wade's empire was about to peak, and he shunned Driesell. Two more Dunbar graduates, Reggie Williams and David Wingate, were featured among Georgetown's 1984 NCAA champions, and Hoyas jackets and T-shirts outnumbered Terps gear on the city's streets. Terrapin Club members seethed over the 1986 hiring of Wade, and the standoff resumed after his ouster in 1989.

Driesell is a southern man who held on to his Washington Redskins season tickets after he left Maryland, and still says, "I love the Redskins." Williams is a Jersey guy who knew he had to build a bridge to Baltimore, where he found considerable resentment when he initially came calling. College Park's part in the conspiracy of segregation included a landmark 1934 lawsuit in which an African American from Baltimore won admission to the university's law school. The plaintiff was represented by Thurgood Marshall, a graduate of Baltimore's Douglass High who went on to become the first African American to sit on the U.S. Supreme Court. Even though Marshall had never applied to Maryland, his not attending the university was among the sins Williams found himself having to beg forgiveness for.

"You couldn't recruit in Baltimore, that was the word when I got here," Williams said. "There was a feeling that Bob Wade was mistreated. Ernie Graham's career was thrown in my face. So was the fact that Thurgood Marshall was not accepted at Maryland. He wouldn't have been accepted at any school south of Baltimore, but we took the blame for that. I spoke to a group of Baltimore businessmen, and I was told that. Even with all of that, there were eras when the University of Maryland simply did not do a good job of going after Baltimore and its alumni."

The antipathy toward Maryland was palpable, from Baltimore in general and Dunbar specifically. "I don't remember Maryland coming into Baltimore as much as they went into D.C.," Pompey said of a recruiting philosophy that dated to Bud Millikan. "The university should have been coming to get our players en masse, and it was a strained relationship. I didn't appreciate how Bob Wade was let go, and many people in Baltimore expressed that same concern. There was resistance to Gary Williams, but he didn't have anything to do with the dismissal of Bob Wade. I asked Keith Booth to make sure he looked at other opportunities, like Duke, but I also told him he couldn't go wrong at Maryland."

Jeremiah Dickens, a family friend, advised Booth to reblaze the 35 miles between Dunbar and College Park. Booth left Maryland as a third-team All-American, but paid immediate dividends for the Terps. A year behind Booth at Dunbar, Rodney Elliott followed him to Maryland and developed into a solid power forward on a Sweet 16 team. For all of the focus on a rift between Baltimore's public schools and the Terps, Maryland historically had even less success recruiting in Baltimore's Catholic League, when it produced national-caliber players like Quintin Dailey and Duane Ferrell. After Gene Shue went to Maryland in 1950, the Terps wouldn't sign a player directly out of a Baltimore Catholic school until 1996, when a slight senior at Calvert Hall named Juan Dixon followed Booth's lead.

Booth's signing elicited national commentary about a warming trend between Maryland and the state's biggest pool of talent, but Williams and his staff were just as excited with the rest of their class. Matt Kovarik was a heady guard from Greensboro, North Carolina, and then there was the stealth recruit. The *Parade* High School All-America team put Booth on its second ten and Smith on the third level. A lean 6-9 center from Norfolk, Virginia, Smith was enamored of Walt Williams, and the Terp coaching staff repaid his interest by latching on to him in 1991 and never letting go. Smith had a solid low-post game, but he didn't get to show it much on the Amateur Athletic Union (AAU) circuit the summer before his junior year. While the star of that AAU team was Allen Iverson, Williams noted Smith's stern defensive play. He played bigger than his 200 pounds, but two years later Smith was still flying under the talent radar.

Among basketball writers, few have a sharper eye than *Sports Illustrated*'s Alexander Woolf. In the magazine's preview of the 1993–94 season, he examined the new breed of athletic big men who could run the floor and face the basket, an evolution that would produce players like Kevin Garnett. Woolf profiled a freshman class that included North Carolina's Rasheed Wallace, Marcus Camby at Massachusetts, and Wisconsin's Rashard Griffith. He noted Darnell Robinson of Arkansas, Duke's Joey Beard and Greg Newton, and Southern California's Avondre Jones. No mention was made of Smith, who had a common name and an uncommon array of skills that enabled him to handle any match-up and prosper in most.

Exree Hipp, Duane Simpkins, and Johnny Rhodes were sophomores when Booth and Smith came to campus. All that youth was picked to finish seventh in the ACC, but just being on a floor with Smith bolstered the confidence of the holdovers who had been beaten down during a 1992–93 season in which they had won just two conference games. With Smith at center and Booth at power forward, Hipp was free to get out on the fast break and Rhodes to cheat into passing lanes for steals. It made

Keith Booth was an intense competitor who stood his ground against opponents a head taller. Because of the doors he opened in Baltimore, Gary Williams considers Booth his most important recruit. (Baltimore Sun.)

for an intriguing mix in practice, but would it fly in an ACC that had produced the last three NCAA champions?

An affirmative hint came in Maryland's very first game. The Georgetown-Maryland rivalry was stopped after the 1979–80 season, done in by angry words between John Thompson and Driesell. The Hoyas had taken over the Washington area with their 1984 NCAA championship, and passed on playing the Terps during three years of the ACC–Big East Challenge. With Russ Potts doing the promotional bidding, Georgetown agreed to open the 1993–94 season against Maryland at the USAir Arena, the Hoyas' home away from home in Landover. Georgetown was coming off a disappointing season in which it had missed the NCAA tournament for the first time in 15 years, but the Hoyas had Othella Harrington and stature that the Terps envied.

"At a mall ten minutes from campus, at all the athletic stores, Maryland was nowhere to be found," Simpkins said. "I got up the nerve and asked one teller, 'Where are your Maryland hats?' He said Maryland hasn't won anything. People were accustomed to seeing us getting blown out."

On November 26, 1993, the day after Thanksgiving, Georgetown felt content when it opened up a 14-point lead with less than 13 minutes remaining. The Terps fought back, however, and the Hoyas needed a late three-pointer to force an overtime. Down a point, Maryland got a steal from reserve forward Kurtis Shultz to set up what would be the biggest basket of Simpkins's career. Simpkins had missed 11 of his first 13 shots and was supposed to get the ball inside to Smith, but he drove past Don Reid and scored for an 84-83 victory. It symbolized two programs' passing in the night. Thompson never scheduled Maryland again, and he got past the first weekend of the NCAA tournament just once more before retiring in 1999. Smith scored 26 points, the most ever in a Maryland debut, and signaled a rebirth that rushed the Terps back into the Sweet 16 in each of his two collegiate seasons.

In 1993–94, Smith became the third freshman to be voted first-team all-ACC, treading where only Clemson's Wise and Georgia Tech's Kenny Anderson had gone, in 1974–75 and 1989–90, respectively. He anchored an ACC All-Rookie team that may never be matched, as it included Wallace and Jerry Stackhouse from North Carolina, and Wake Forest's Tim Duncan. In 1994–95, Smith joined South Carolina's John Roche, N.C. State's David Thompson, and Virginia's Ralph Sampson in an elite club, sophomores who were named ACC Player of the Year.

Smith accelerated the timetable for Maryland's rebuilding project, but the Terps' material still wasn't up to the standards at the top of the conference. In Smith's freshman season, Grant Hill carried Duke to the NCAA championship game. North Carolina won the ACC tournament, and the Tar Heels posed serious match-up problems for the Terps. En route to the NCAA title the previous season, North Carolina had pounded Maryland by an average of 26 points. The Tar Heels had a 7-footer in Kevin Salvadori, but he looked tiny compared with Eric Montross, who was 7-0 and 258 pounds. Williams's staff fretted over that front line until Booth spoke up. Put Joe on Salvadori, he said, and let me take Montross, who had six inches and nearly 50 pounds on Booth. The Terps didn't beat the Tar Heels that season, but they played them tough, and those who weren't already Booth fans got in his corner.

"I've never had a more courageous player," Williams recalled during a time when he had Dixon. "Let the truth be said, Keith's 6-4, even though we used to list him at 6-5 or 6-6. He never doubted what he could do, that he could rebound, defend, and score against a big tree like Montross."

Those Terps lost 7 of their last 11 regular-season games and had some anxiety on Selection Sunday, but they earned a berth in the NCAA tournament for the first time since 1988. Unfazed by a tenth seed in the Midwest Regional, they barged into Wichita, Kansas, and handled a smaller Saint Louis team in the first round, then avenged a 14-point loss with an upset of second-seeded Massachusetts. Michigan stopped Cinderella in a Sweet 16 game in Dallas, but the Terps had a satisfying season and a promising future. In November 1994, Williams signed a seven-year contract extension, and the Terps began the second—and last—season of the Joe Smith era.

Maryland began the 1994–95 campaign ranked No. 7, its first preseason Top 10 recognition since 1983–84. The Terps dropped the championship game of the Maui Invitational to Arizona State, and Simpkins was inconsolable two weeks later, after a loss to Massachusetts at the Baltimore Arena. In one of the wildest ACC seasons ever, Maryland was one of four teams to go 12-4 and share regular-season honors, and the Terps' clincher was unforgettable.

As Maryland prepared for its March 1 game at Duke, Blue Devil coach Mike Krzyzewski was on leave with a back injury and Williams wasn't feeling well himself. Assistant coach Billy Hahn and J. J. Bush, who has worked into his fourth decade as a Maryland trainer, knew something was wrong when Williams missed practice the day before the game. There was a chartered flight waiting to take the Terps to Raleigh-Durham International Airport, and Bush went to Williams's home to drive him to Baltimore Washington International.

"When I got to his house, he looked horrible," Bush said. "I took his temperature and pulse, and told him he was too sick to travel. When he quit fighting me, I knew it was serious. He was transported to the hospital and treated for double pneumonia. His lungs were so filled with fluid. The doctors let me know that if it had been another 24 hours, we wouldn't have had this conversation."

With Williams on antibiotics and wavering in and out of consciousness, Hahn called the shots at Duke. The Blue Devils were struggling through a 13-18 season that led Krzyzewski to appeal to the NCAA to have all but the 9-3 start he had attended to stricken from his permanent record, and the game plan was simple: Get the ball inside to Smith. The Terps hadn't won at Cameron Indoor Stadium since 1988, and when Smith tipped in a miss by Simpkins at the buzzer, he finished with a career-high 40 points and 18 rebounds and Maryland had a 94-92 victory. The television audience was treated to an impromptu dance between Hahn and basketball publicist Chuck Walsh.

"That was very emotional," Hahn said. "The next day, people said, 'Can we see you dance?' and I had no idea what they were talking about. Then I saw the tape, and I said, 'What a jerk.' The next morning I went to the hospital to see Gary, and he didn't even know we had won. He was still out of it. People have no idea how seriously ill Gary was."

Smith's teammates cooed, "I want to be like Joe," but the momentum was short-lived. A win at Virginia would have given the Terps the regular-season title outright, but they lost by 25. Williams spent his 50th birthday at Washington Adventist Hospital and missed the ACC tournament, and Maryland never regained its edge. The Terps had probably

After years in hiding, it really wasn't necessary for Terp fans to take on disguises once Gary Williams guided Maryland back to the NCAA tournament. (Maryland Sports Information.)

peaked on February 7, when Simpkins and Rhodes shot a combined 16-for-23 from the field and Smith collected 14 points and 16 rebounds in an 86-73 conquest of No. 1 North Carolina, but the Tar Heels got revenge in the ACC tournament semifinals. Williams was allowed to travel with his team to the NCAA tournament, but only if he promised to follow Bush's regimen of fluids and rest. Seeded third in the West Regional, the Terps toyed with Gonzaga and Texas in Salt Lake City, but met their match in Oakland, California, where Connecticut and Ray Allen beat them, 99-89. The Huskies were second seeded, so it wasn't an upset on the NCAA bracket, but Williams rates it among the most devastating postseason losses he's ever endured. "We didn't play a very good game," Williams said. "I felt we didn't compete."

Smith had purchased a $1 million insurance policy the previous summer, and Williams's pain was exacerbated by the knowledge that his landmark big man was ready to go pro. Mister Smith came to Washington and collected 1,290 points and 683 rebounds in just two seasons, numbers that projected to nearly 2,600 and 1,400 over a four-year career. Most important to long-suffering Terp fans, he won, and no one blamed him for going to the NBA.

ON JANUARY 23, 2002, Maryland was supposed to be tested on the road by a good Wake Forest team. The Terps piled up a big lead in Winston-Salem, however, and Dick Vitale felt compelled to hold on to an ESPN audience that had its thumb on the remote control. The game wasn't worth dissecting, so Vitale's ramblings took him to what he considered Maryland's all-time top five: A front line of Len Elmore, Buck Williams, and Tom McMillen, with Len Bias shifting into the backcourt alongside John Lucas. Mike Patrick, ESPN's play-by-play man, remarked how he disliked that kind of armchair talk, then offered a rebuttal in behalf of Joe Smith. No mention was made of Steve Francis, maybe the most spectacular Terp ever to fly through Cole.

Twenty-five days later, when Maryland dismantled No. 1 Duke, there were scattered objections over the pregame ceremony, at which an oversized No. 23 jersey was unfurled from the Cole rafters, immortalizing Francis alongside the 15 of Lucas, the 34 of Bias, and uniforms of other Terp greats. Terence Morris and others with more substantial career accomplishments had not received the honor, and Gary Williams reiterated that All-America status was the criterion.

Francis had been a second-team selection in 1998–99, the only season he spent in Maryland, but his impact on the Terps went far beyond a 17.0-point scoring average and a sour NCAA tournament. His entrance electrified Midnight Madness, as he bounded down from the Cole concourse to the court that would become his launching pad. His exit was an ugly night in Knoxville, Tennessee, when he trash-talked his way through a pitiful loss to St. John's. In those five short months, Francis kept Maryland's name in the national consciousness at a time when basketball was not in favor throughout the land.

Francis filled a vacuum, and gave Maryland star power it had lacked since Smith's departure.

In the spring of 1995, Williams gave his blessing to Smith's plans to enter the draft. The decision was a no-brainer, as the lanky sophomore was the No. 1 selection. Maryland had four returning starters and was tabbed No. 15 in the 1995–96 preseason poll, but the Terps immediately came back to the middle of the pack in the Atlantic Coast Conference. The players were disheartened to discover how much better they had been when Smith was drawing triple teams and covering their backs. Keith Booth had a splendid junior season. Johnny Rhodes went out in style, as he averaged 16.7 points and 5.9 rebounds and set an ACC career record with his 344th steal, but the rest of the senior class did not distinguish itself.

A 51.4 percent shooter when Smith had triggered the fast break and merited so much attention in the half-court offense, Exree Hipp made just 36.8 percent of his attempts as a senior. Leadership became an issue for both of Maryland's revenue programs, as the quarterback and point guard didn't supply the direction associated with those positions. The Terps' football team imploded in 1995, when Scott Milanovich returned from a four-game NCAA suspension for gambling and disrupted the chemistry of a 4-0 start. As skilled as Milanovich was, his return marked the beginning of the end for coach Mark Duffner. Three months after the football team stumbled to the finish and extended its bowl drought to five years, Duane Simpkins had to serve a three-game suspension when the more than $8,000 in campus parking fines that he had accumulated were paid for in part by his Amateur Athletic Union coach, a violation of NCAA rules. The Hipp-Simpkins-Rhodes class exited in Tempe, Arizona, with a meek upset loss in the first round of the NCAA tournament to Santa Clara, which had the best player on the floor, guard Steve Nash.

The seniors moved on, to the delight of a freshman class that itched for more playing time. Terrell Stokes, who had been North Carolina star Rasheed Wallace's setup man at Simon Gratz High in Philadelphia, inherited the point guard position from Simpkins. On the wing, Rhodes begat Laron Profit, who fancied himself the best player ever out of Delaware. The claim wasn't all boast. In the middle, center Obinna Ekezie continued to shed his baby fat and expand his basketball knowledge.

Ekezie gave the Terps a second foreign-born starter, although both he and junior guard Sarunas Jasikevicius had played high school basketball in the United States. Jasikevicius was from Lithuania, and in 2000 he would nearly provide the biggest story of the Summer Olympics in Sydney, Australia. By then one of the best point guards in Europe, Jasikevicius outplayed Jason Kidd and Gary Payton from the American "Dream Team" in a semifinal game. A quarter of a mile away in Olympic Park, hundreds of American reporters tired of writing about track and field star Marion Jones cheered Jasikevicius, whose three-pointer at the buzzer was altered by Antonio McDyess.

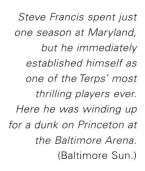

Steve Francis spent just one season at Maryland, but he immediately established himself as one of the Terps' most thrilling players ever. Here he was winding up for a dunk on Princeton at the Baltimore Arena. (Baltimore Sun.)

Six years earlier, Jasikevicius had come to College Park with a strong fundamental background. A year later, Ekezie came in lacking even rudimentary skills. He was teased about everything from his weight to his middle name, Ralph, which just didn't seem to fit a man from Port Harcourt, Nigeria. Ekezie studied engineering and economics, and silenced his teammates with the reminder, "I speak the King's English."

Booth earned first-team all-ACC status in 1996–97, when he averaged career highs of 19.5 points and 7.9 rebounds and taught all those new starters how to play hard. Unburdened by a preseason ranking, the Terps matched the school record with an 11-0 start that Georgia ended in the championship game of the Rainbow Classic in Honolulu. Maryland bounced right back with an upset win at North Carolina, and 11 days later it continued to shake up the ACC, when Profit's long jumper handed Tim Duncan a rare loss at Wake Forest. The Terps' seven-man rotation hit the wall in February, however, as they lost six of their last nine regular-season ACC games.

Profit and Stokes broke curfew after a first-round blowout of Clemson in the ACC tournament in Greensboro, and both were benched when Maryland began the NCAA tournament in Memphis, Tennessee. Other disciplinary problems at Maryland were few and suspensions nonexistent over the next five years. His players stayed off the police blotter, but Williams was criticized over his players' graduation rate, which, under the NCAA's methodology, dipped to 13.3 percent in 1999.

The Terps' first-round match-up in the 1997 tournament typified the bias that the NCAA men's basketball committee shows toward teams from major conferences. The College of Charleston was ranked 16th and had a computer rating higher than that of Maryland, which was No. 22 in the Associated Press rankings. The C of C was seeded 12th, however, and Williams fretted over a pairing that seeded his team fifth. Booth's career ended in a nine-point loss that left him with 916 rebounds and a patriotic 1,776 points. He wore red and white, and left the opposition black and blue.

Booth's departure left an opening at power forward, and Rodney Elliott filled it in 1997–98 with a solid game that showed he had outgrown the nickname "Noodles," a remnant from an adolescence in which he had been painfully thin. Elliott's splendid senior season kept a talented freshman from Frederick in a reserve role, and that was just fine with Morris, who preferred a methodical pace.

When Morris had been in the seventh grade, he hadn't started for Monocacy Middle School. In 1995, when he was a sophomore at Thomas Johnson High, his block lifted the Patriots into the state Class 3A championship game at Cole. Two weeks into his junior year, Morris announced that he would play collegiate ball for Maryland. He was interested in North Carolina, but his mother had her hands full running a large, single-parent household, and he had clicked at a summer camp with Matt Hahn, whose father, Billy, was Williams's right-hand man. Morris was 6-8, had a soft shooting touch, and moved with grace, but Thomas Johnson did not get back to Cole when he was a junior. Coach Tom Dickman saw that the Patriots just weren't tough enough, and when Morris finally got a state title in 1997, it helped that TJ had added Randall Jones, who would become an all-ACC honorable-mention safety for Maryland's football team during its magical 2001 season.

In 1997–98, Morris was mixed into an intriguing bunch. The Terps knocked off a Kansas team that included Paul Pierce and Raef LaFrentz in the semifinals of the Franklin National Bank Classic at the new MCI Center. The next day they lost to George Washington when Stokes couldn't handle Shawnta Rogers, a 5-3 guard out of Baltimore in the Muggsy Bogues mold. That loss dropped Maryland to 4-3, and expectations weren't all that high five weeks later, when top-ranked North Carolina came to Cole.

In a transfer of power that displayed his influence in Chapel Hill, North Carolina coach Dean Smith waited until October, a few days before the start of practice, to announce his retirement. Loyal lieutenant Bill Guthridge was elevated to the top spot, and the Tar Heels didn't miss a beat. With Vince Carter doing his Michael Jordan imitation and point guard Ed Cota feeding the ball to Antawn Jamison in the low post, North Carolina cruised into College Park on January 14, 1998, with a 17-0 record. It left with an 89-83 overtime loss and a Cole memory as vivid as any for longtime radio play-by-play man Johnny Holliday, as Morris chipped in ten points and freshman classmate Mike Mardesich had what would be the best game of his career. Against Williams's wishes, the 7-footer had red-shirted the previous season, but Mardesich was hailed as a hero when he collected 12 points, nine rebounds, and the basket that sent the game into overtime. Once there, Profit took care of business.

That Maryland team was often greater than the sum of its parts, but it had a fragile psyche and folded when confronted with a Duke uniform. Mardesich struggled with his shot throughout his career, as he turned dunks into lay-ins and lay-ins into fade-away jumpers. Profit was equally introspective, and suffered from paralysis by analysis. The more he thought about his shooting stroke, the worse it got, and Greg Manning, the former Terp shooting ace who did the radio color during Profit's career, took him aside in Puerto Rico in 1998 and told him to stop short-arming his release.

Stokes was one Terp with a hardened shell. He spent part of his youth in a court-adjudicated school, and told cautionary tales about selling drugs. When Williams benched him midway through his junior season, Stokes was left to figure it out on his own. He did, and directed Maryland to ten wins in the ACC and a heated rematch with North Carolina in the tournament semifinals. Maryland lost to still–No. 1 North Carolina, but not before the Tar Heels needed a dubious hand-check call by referee Larry Rose against Jasikevicius to extend the Terps into overtime. Ekezie provided a hilarious highlight that seemed inspired by a bad western, as he strode the length of the floor at the Greensboro Coliseum and stared down Tar Heel fans before he completed a three-point play.

Ekezie's clutch free-throw shooting beat Illinois in the second round of the NCAA tournament in Sacramento, California, but the Terps lacked the talent to stay with defending champion Arizona in their West Regional semifinal.

Thwarted at the round of 16 again, Maryland needed a dynamic player, one who could generate the kind of national attention that a Carter brought to North Carolina. Enter Francis.

Tony Massenburg made the Memphis Grizzlies his tenth NBA team in 2001–2. Francis was nearly as well traveled, as Maryland had become his sixth school in as many years in 1998. His talent was evident, his background murky. Francis claimed that the death of his mother had left him too distraught to think about basketball at Montgomery Blair in 1994–95, but in fact Brenda Wilson succumbed to cancer after what would have been his senior season at the high school in Silver Spring, a few miles from College Park. An indifferent approach to school work was one reason his high school career had consisted of one season as a reserve, when he was a sophomore at Blair. He had been academically ineligible to play there as a freshman, but made the varsity as a sophomore, when he said that schools from Bullis Prep to St. John's Prospect Hall in Frederick made a run at him. As a junior, he transferred to John F. Kennedy High but broke an ankle. When he went back to Blair for his senior year, Montgomery County transfer rules prohibited his participation. Dale Lamberth, the Blair coach, said, "There were times when I thought he was just going to be a superstar in the ghetto."

Francis got his general equivalency diploma and enrolled at Milford Academy in Connecticut, but left that basketball finishing school after one semester. In 1996, he prepared to follow his friend Jason Miskiri to Montgomery-Rockville, but instead enrolled at one of the nation's junior college powers. San Jacinto in Texas was a place to play and shore up shaky academic backgrounds. Baltimoreans Sam Cassell and Michael Lloyd had gone there, and so had Stacy Robinson when he was unable to make the jump from DuVal High to Maryland. Francis guided "San Jac" to the national finals, then abruptly left Texas and returned to Maryland. He transferred to Allegany Community College in Cumberland, where coach Bob Kirk had turned a remote location in western Maryland into a haven.

Francis was as charismatic as basketball players come. When Louis Goldstein, the late state comptroller, visited Allegany on official business, he asked to meet Francis. Clearly shorter than his listed 6-foot-3, Francis

Thanks to Steve Francis, the 1998–99 Terps were a fun group to watch. Gary Williams loosened up with Francis on the bench near the end of an ACC tournament rout of Florida State, but that postseason soon turned sour. (Baltimore Sun.)

could not be intimidated, as he had been hardened by playing with his older brothers and their friends had run him into the walls at Piney Branch Elementary in Takoma Park during pick-up games. When he was little more than five feet tall and trying to play high school football at Blair, a coach there took to calling him "Little Shit." He was fearless, slick off the dribble, and willing to distribute the ball to his teammates. Francis announced that he would come to Maryland in 1998, but that was a cautious spring, because he toyed with the idea of entering the NBA draft.

Francis groomed himself to the play point guard in the pros. Maryland already had a capable one in Stokes, so Williams was faced with delicate matters regarding his rotation. Francis showed up late for the first exhibition, and a lightly regarded redshirt freshman named Juan Dixon started in his place against the Aussie All-Stars, but Francis quickly became a constant. He could throw an alley-oop pass to Profit or Morris for a dunk, or be on the other end. He led that high-wire act to a ridiculously easy run through the Puerto Rico Shootout, and played brilliantly against Stanford in the BB&T Classic on December 6, when an odd message first appeared among the homemade signs: "Fear the Turtle." Washington College graduate Drew Elburn was a Terps fan who could not have envisioned how his slogan would catch on.

Maryland took a 10-0 record to Kentucky's Rupp Arena, where its quest for the program's first No. 1 ranking was blocked. Every time Francis took the ball to the basket, which was nearly every time he touched it, Jamaal Magloire knocked him to the floor. Francis and Morris led a fine comeback, but the Terps lost a shootout, 103-91.

John Nash, general manager of the New Jersey Nets, said Francis could be the No. 1 choice in the 1999 NBA draft, and Terp fans understood that they had better enjoy him while they had the chance. Francis had a peaceful coexistence with the seniors who had gone to the Sweet 16 the previous season. He took away scoring chances for Profit, the other wing, but made a star out of Morris, who had the best field-goal percentage of his career and joined Francis on the all-ACC first team. On January 24 at Clemson, Maryland ran a double screen for Morris, whose 15-foot jump shot sealed an overtime win. A week later, the Terps suffered through two desultory losses at Wake Forest and Duke, and Williams took a radical step.

Usually loyal to his seniors and hesitant to start freshmen, Williams shook up his team by benching Ekezie, who had been rebounding poorly, and inserting Lonny Baxter at center. Both played well in a romp over Virginia, but the move became fraught with guilt three days later, when Ekezie tore his Achilles tendon in practice a few hours before the Terps were to board a waiting bus behind Cole and begin a trip to N.C. State. Maryland won its next six games but missed Ekezie in the postseason.

The Terps were lost offensively against North Carolina in the semifinals of the ACC tournament. In the third round of the NCAAs, St. John's pushed the Terps away from the basket, and Maryland suffered through a ten-minute scoring drought and a 76-62 setback. At least Ekezie would have been good for a trip to the free-throw line in that hideous stretch, when the Terps were bullied. Just as Providence's Marvin Barnes had intimidated Tom McMillen in 1973, Ron Artest pushed around Morris. Francis talked trash to the end, as he told the St. John's guards that when they were playing college ball the next season, he would be making millions in the NBA. It was an unpleasant farewell, but it did not diminish the influence Francis had in his short stay with the Terps.

Francis burst onto the Maryland scene during a walkout by NBA players. Needing someplace to feed their "Basketball Jones," the league's executives and coaches flocked to see Francis. He became a staple on ESPN's "Sports Center," and the media circus at Maryland became even wilder when the Terps offered a scholarship to Tamir Goodman, an Orthodox Jew from Baltimore. Prospects with more traditional backgrounds, but from out-of-the-way places, noticed Maryland, too. Byron Mouton, the disgruntled leading scorer at Tulane University, watched Francis as he made plans to leave New Orleans. In Whiteville, North Carolina, a raw, young forward named Chris Wilcox followed Francis's exuberant play and thought he might look good in a Terps uniform, too.

18

COLLEGE PUBLICISTS ARE ALWAYS on the lookout for a pithy catch phrase with which to market a Heisman Trophy campaign in football or an All-America bid in basketball. Near the end of their college careers Lonny Baxter and Juan Dixon were dubbed "Thunder and Lightning," but neither was forecast to alter the conditions at Maryland as much as they did.

In 1998, Baxter was an afterthought at Hargrave Military Academy. His powerful frame and low-post moves excited the Maryland staff, but he wasn't the top recruit at that prep school in Virginia. Baxter wasn't even the best frontcourt player at Hargrave, where classmate Korleone Young filed for early entry in the NBA draft and was taken with the 40th pick by the Detroit Pistons. Baxter was as unassuming as a 6-foot-8, 270-pound center can be—the nameplate on his locker was misspelled "Lonnie" for his first two seasons at Maryland—but he slimmed down his build, beefed up his game, and became one of the Terps' best big men ever.

What about Dixon? Gary Williams took some heat for offering him a scholarship, and even the Terp coach didn't envision that Dixon would do the seemingly impossible on Easter Week in 2002. Dixon didn't just upstage the Baltimore Orioles in Opening Day festivities at Camden Yards; he also overshadowed the Washington Wizards' news that Michael Jordan's career might finally be done for good. It wasn't enough that Dixon ended decades of frustration and led Maryland to its first NCAA basketball championship; his was the most poignant success story Terp athletics had ever produced. When the circumstances of his upbringing were juxtaposed against the backgrounds of the two players whose legacies he chased and passed, Dixon's story became more inspirational, theirs more painful to retell.

Maryland basketball fans are more familiar than most with the ravages of drug abuse and addiction. Len Bias raised the Terps' all-time scoring record to 2,149 points in March 1986; three months later, a cocaine overdose ended not just a promising pro career, but also his life. Bias's rise to college stardom coincided with the unraveling of John Lucas's

NBA career, as Maryland's first three-time all-ACC selection became addicted to cocaine, which sapped his mental and physical strength when he should have been at the peak of his powers. Bias didn't survive drugs. Lucas and other Maryland players did. While Dixon's story warmed the heart of anyone with a soft spot for the underdog, people with personal experience in dealing with demons watched him develop and shook their heads in amazement, as he became maybe the most accomplished Terps player ever.

When Dixon accepted a scholarship offer from Maryland in October 1996, talent scout Tom Konchalski led the chorus of skeptics who said, "He's got to get a lot stronger." Doubts about his ability to make it in the Atlantic Coast Conference didn't subside despite a solid senior season, as Dixon hadn't weighed more than 150 pounds when he graduated from Calvert Hall, a Catholic high school for boys located in the Baltimore suburb of Towson. The men and women who raised him, however, understood that the intangible qualities Dixon possessed were more important than numbers on a roster.

By the end of Dixon's sophomore year at Maryland, he had grown tired of telling his life story. He was eager to acknowledge the debt he owed his extended family, but in doing so he didn't want to slight his parents. Super Bowl lore includes a litany of stupid questions—Doug Williams of the Washington Redskins was once asked how long he had been a black quarterback—but insensitivity isn't limited to football. A writer in a rush once posed this icebreaker to Dixon: Did your parents live in a crack house?

Juan Dixon was 4 years old and big brother Phil 8 when they went to live with their maternal grandmother in northeast Baltimore. Their parents tried to be discreet about their habits, but both had descended into heroin addiction and were incapable of providing a stable home environment. Their drug abuse would lead to AIDS and early death, as Juanita, his mother, succumbed to the disease just as Dixon was entering his sophomore year at a new high school. In December of Dixon's junior year, AIDS took his father, Phil Sr. By then, Juan had learned to stand on his own, albeit with more than a little help from his family and friends.

Filmmaker Barry Levinson had romanticized Baltimore in movies like *Diner, Tin Men,* and *Avalon,* but he also introduced the nation to the seamier side of the city, as producer of the television series *Homicide.* The cop drama was inspired by the police-beat reporting of David Simon, whose book *The Corner* and the series it inspired on HBO chronicled the drug trade and its victims in and around a West Baltimore intersection. There were about 50,000 junkies' stories to tell, as the federal govern-

Before every free throw, Juan Dixon touched his chest to remind himself of his late mother, Juanita, and the family losses that he had endured en route to becoming a star uplifted by considerable inner strength. (Baltimore Sun.)

ment estimated that 1 in every 12 Baltimore City residents was a heroin addict. The epidemic's resultant crime and violence endangered innocent citizens and became fodder for angry white males. On conservative talk shows, callers wanted to know: Why can't more inner city youth turn out like Juan Dixon?

His circumstances might have been common, but Dixon's extended family was not. After his brother Phil became the all-time leading scorer at Shenandoah College, a Virginia school that plays at the NCAA's Division III level, he became a police officer in the city. Juan's vast support system of aunts and uncles included Sheila Dixon, who would become the city council president, one of the most powerful officeholders in Baltimore. The clan included heroes like Mark Smith, Sheila's former husband, who shepherded Phil and Juan into sports and away from dealers who wanted to recruit the boys as runners. All that love and direction made Dixon's youth as normal as possible, but he displayed extraordinary grit.

Dixon quarterbacked youth football teams in the Northeast Baltimore neighborhoods of Gardenville and Overlea, and one coach allowed him to call his own plays before he was 10. Tagging along with Phil, trying to keep up with boys four years older and more, made him smarter and tougher than most kids his age.

"I was coaching Phil's Little League baseball team, and Juan was 8 or 9, too young to play," Smith said. "Juan was our batboy, and a line-drive foul ball hit him right in the eye. I was getting ready to rush him to the hospital, but he didn't cry at all. He might have said ouch."

At Calvert Hall, Dixon had many run-ins with Mark Amatucci, the coach who had used inner-city talent to bring the Cardinals a mythical national championship in 1982. Amatucci was used to dealing with street-smart kids. Dixon was as tough as any, but when he went through the motions against inferior players, Amatucci benched him. Dixon began to take inferior players seriously, but he still lived for the big game. Featuring Baxter, Anacostia High was ranked No. 1 by the *Washington Post* during the 1996–97 season, but Calvert Hall pulled off an upset when they met, thanks to 47 points by Dixon. Fans critical of Williams's recruiting strategy nonetheless wanted Albert Mouring, who went from Colonel Richardson on Maryland's Eastern Shore to Connecticut, and said that Dixon was a mistake.

Finding a niche was harder in the classroom than on a basketball court. Dixon once said he had never read a book cover to cover before he entered Calvert Hall, and he had serious trouble fulfilling the academic requirements necessary for freshman eligibility in Division I of the NCAA. A low grade-point average meant that he needed to post a score of 930 on the SAT, and there was shouting and crying as Dixon took the standardized test a half dozen times before his result soared to 1,060. His previous scores had ranged from 820 down to 690, and the sudden jump raised a red flag with SAT administrators, who ignored the documented work that Dixon had done with tutors and disallowed the score that would have allowed him to play for Maryland in the 1997–98 season. By the time Dixon got a qualifying SAT result that wasn't questioned, the Terps had been practicing for a month and he had spent the fall semester working a job at Baltimore's Inner Harbor.

After he got his good SAT news, Dixon had to wait a month before he could join the Terps, at the conclusion of the fall semester. With Sarunas Jasikevicius and Laron Profit logging long minutes at the wing positions, the Terps could have used Dixon, but Williams decided against burning a full year of Dixon's eligibility and he was redshirted. Instead of working with the regular rotation, Dixon watched video of upcoming opponents and mimicked Georgia Tech's Dion Glover, North Carolina's Shammond Williams, and other top ACC guards in practice. He enjoyed a pressure-free semester, in retrospect one of the best things that ever happened to him.

Maryland added two guards to its roster in 1998–99, and both were hungry. While Dixon got four and a half seasons to make his mark at Maryland, Steve Francis was on campus for one year, and his intensity made an impression on Dixon. Both were scorers raised by extended families, but Francis was a playmaker who operated best with the ball, while Dixon would run all game to get it. Their physiques were as different as their styles, but if track and field coaches had recruited the two, the United States might have a bigger international profile in the long jump and the 800 meters. Francis is a collection of coiled muscle, with the explosive speed and bounding ability that would have made him a world-class jumper. Dixon has the wide shoulders and low percentage of body fat common to endurance athletes.

While the entire nation knew about Francis, Williams immediately took a liking to the skinny rookie with all the aunts and uncles, the origin of the poster slogan "All for Juan, Juan for All." Williams said Dixon was the one player he couldn't scare. The coach's life had been turned upside down when his parents separated. The player's parents hadn't just broken up, they had died, and the trauma Dixon and Williams had experienced as teenagers created a unique bond between them. "We understand what the other went through," Dixon said toward the end of his Maryland career. "He's a tough individual, and I am also. He loves coaching, I love playing this game. We get along well."

Williams's admiration for Dixon soared in the 1999–2000 season, when the sophomore guard's stellar play cooled some of the controversy over Maryland's handling of another Baltimorean. In January 1999, even Francis had been eclipsed by the media frenzy that followed the news that Williams would give a scholarship to Tamir Goodman, an Orthodox Jew whose faith prohibited him from playing on the Sabbath, sundown Friday to sundown Saturday. Goodman was in his junior year at Talmudical Academy, and within days the obscure little school for boys was being visited by reporters from *Sports Illustrated* and the *New York Times* and camera crews from *60 Minutes*. All wanted to interview "the Jewish Jordan."

Goodman had an injury-marred summer and transferred to Takoma Academy, a Seventh-Day Adventist school near College Park. Williams began to second-guess his offer, and had a contentious meeting with Goodman's mother on September 2. Williams said he wasn't sure that Goodman was capable of making an impact in the ACC; Chava Goodman contended that the Sabbath was the issue. As Goodman went to New York to observe Rosh Hashanah, the Jewish New Year, he announced that he would not sign a letter of intent to attend Maryland.

Williams preferred to take a public relations hit earlier rather than later, which would have been the case if Goodman had enrolled at Maryland and left the basketball team as he did at Towson University during the 2001–2 season, but within months media and fans had another Baltimorean to write and talk about.

As frail as he was thought to be, Dixon was ready for stardom when Francis and Profit moved on in 1999. Terence Morris was the ACC's only returning first-team all-star, but Matt Hahn was Maryland's only senior and the Terps were not in the Top 25 when that 1999–2000 season began. Baxter didn't establish himself as a force until the midseason, but Dixon showed from day one that he would assume the role if Morris was uncomfortable as the go-to player.

In his first three games as a Maryland starter, Dixon scored 71 points. He shot miserably in the fourth, but still wanted the ball at the end against Kentucky at Madison Square Garden. Two weeks later, Dixon's jumper from the right baseline with 6.3 seconds left beat Illinois in the championship game of the BB&T Classic. With freshman Steve Blake at the point, the youthful Terps were inconsistent, as they dropped the championship game of that tournament at the MCI Center to George Washington. Morris starred at Cole against Kentucky, but Maryland began ACC play with three straight losses. Most dispiriting was an 80-70 setback to Duke at Cole in which Maryland suffered from its customary stage fright against the Blue Devils. With the big three of Baxter, Dixon, and Morris combining to make only 19 of their 56 field-goal attempts, the Terps' shooting percentage was a shaky .341.

The offense was just as ineffectual at North Carolina, and at practice the next day in Tallahassee, where they were preparing for Florida State, the Terps spent hours doing little but pounding the ball inside to Baxter. Maryland won its next two, but the second Duke week unfolded shakily. With the Terps in danger of falling to 4-5 in the conference, Baxter willed them to a pivotal win over N.C. State. Maryland whittled a 17-point first-half deficit to five and seized momentum when Baxter, the lone defender against a 3-on-1 fast break, drew an improbable charging foul from Damon Thornton. His dunk waved off, Thornton made an angry outburst and drew a technical. Suffering from cramps, Dixon hit two free throws and a runner in the lane, and Baxter banked in the go-ahead bucket as the Wolfpack continued to collapse. When the burly sophomore hugged and danced with his coach 75 seconds later, it was hard to distinguish who was soaked in more sweat. Williams said it was the best comeback he had been associated with in 30 years, but it wouldn't be his most memorable victory of the week.

When the Terps went to Cameron Indoor Stadium on February 9, 2000, Duke seemed invincible despite its youngest team ever. A season removed from a loss in the NCAA championship game to Connecticut and Richard Hamilton, and from the early entries to the NBA of William Avery, Elton Brand, and Corey Maggette, the Blue Devils reloaded with a powerful recruiting class. Carlos Boozer, Mike Dunleavy Jr., and Jason Williams clicked with returning starters Chris Carrawell and Shane Battier. Duke had an 18-game winning streak, the nation's best; 31 straight regular season victories against conference competition, an ACC record; and a school-record 46-game run going at Cameron, where Maryland was accustomed to getting blown out.

Williams had never experienced the pleasure of shaking hands with Mike Krzyzewski after a Maryland win in Durham. The Terps had won once at Cameron during the Williams era, but he hadn't been around to enjoy it, as he had been hospitalized with pneumonia when Joe Smith beat a mediocre Blue Devil bunch in 1995. The scenario seemed familiar, as Morris had trouble locating Battier, who hit consecutive three-pointers to give Duke a 33-26 lead, but then Baxter continued his physical play and was in the middle of a run of 11 straight Maryland points.

Battier never cooled off, and his driving basket gave Duke a 79-76 lead, but then Dixon took over the game. He scored from the left baseline, converted a Duke turnover into a transition basket, and then made a play that epitomized his resourcefulness. The Terps freed Morris for a three-pointer on the right wing, but it bounced off the rim and to the left side. Dixon, skinny butt and all, got position on the bigger, stronger, and more experienced Carrawell, who would be voted ACC Player of the Year. Dixon's put-back staggered Duke, and Morris followed with two daggers, as his successive three-pointers gave Maryland and Williams a breakthrough win.

It was the second game that season in which the coach changed his stripes. In the BB&T Classic, Maryland had been in danger of getting blown out by Illinois when Williams realized that his Terps, built on a foundation of running and pressing, couldn't keep up with the Fighting Illini. For one of the few times in his career, Williams slowed the tempo instead of pushing it, and stole a victory. At Duke, one of the most demonstrative coaches in the country was uncommonly serene, and his players were loose and cool. Watching the game on television from his home in Frederick, Tom Dickman, Morris's high school coach, wondered if Williams and Hahn had been sedated before the game.

Maryland turned that week's momentum into a second-place finish in the regular season and its first ACC tournament championship game since 1984, the year Len Bias had performed magic in Greensboro. Danny Miller, the Terps' starting small forward, sprained an ankle in the semifinal win over N.C. State, and his absence was a factor as Maryland fell back in the second half and dropped the championship game to Duke, despite 19 points by Dixon.

Coaches like to flee town as quickly as they can after they are eliminated from losses, and Williams had grown accustomed to watching the NCAA tournament selection show on CBS from Cole. The Duke loss hurt, but discovering its NCAA destination from a hotel in Charlotte instead of its team room eased the sting some. Besides, it was Maryland's only ACC final in its first 13 seasons under Williams. The Terps were rewarded with the No. 3 seed in the Midwest Regional, where a sweet season came to a sour end in the second round. Miller rested his ankle against Iona, but then they ran into UCLA, whose veterans were motivated by the spanking Francis and company had administered in Puerto Rico the season before. Blake shivered afterward with a cold, and his counterpart was red hot, as Earl Watson made five of six three-point tries and notched a UCLA record 16 assists. Several came on 60-foot lob passes, as the Bruins abused the Terps in a 105-70 win that was tied for Maryland's worst postseason loss ever and its most lopsided in any game since 1993.

Williams and his players limped out of the Hubert H. Humphrey Metrodome in Minneapolis. They knew that the next college basketball season would climax there. With every regular planning to return, the Terps vowed to get back to Minnesota and give Maryland its first Final Four team.

19

HOW DO YOU DEVELOP UNITY in teenage mercenaries? Basketball players change high schools as easily as they do hairstyles, and the old college try has become an anachronism in an era when business interests from Nike to drug cartels contract street agents to identify youngsters with NBA potential.

The players that Gary Williams assembled in 2000 were a case in point. The Terps' newcomers included two talented forwards. Byron Mouton was a transfer who had sat out the previous season. In 1999 he had clashed with Tulane coach Perry Clark, and Mouton was painted as a malcontent more interested in his scoring average than the win column. Chris Wilcox, a freshman with enormous potential, had gone to three high schools in North Carolina. As a junior he had led Whiteville, located in the southeastern part of the state, to a state Class 2A championship, then moved to Raleigh at the urgings of an AAU coach and spent his senior season at Enloe High.

Lonny Baxter and Steve Blake were nearly as well traveled as Steve Francis, who had made Maryland his sixth school in as many years. Baxter had spent his junior year of high school at Richard Montgomery in Rockville. In 1996, he had transferred to Anacostia High in the District. Academically ineligible to play immediately in the NCAA, he spent a season at Hargrave Military Academy in Chatham, Virginia. The point guard in charge of giving Maryland a sense of direction, Blake had been all over the South Florida map. After he led Miami Killian to the semifinals of the Florida state tournament, Blake joined Udonis Haslem and other hand-picked talent to lead Miami Senior High to a final national ranking of No. 4. When Florida's High School Activities Association stripped Miami Senior of its 1998 state title and shut down that Nike-funded program over its recruiting practices, Blake moved on to Oak Hill Academy, another prep school in remote southwestern Virginia.

Mike Mardesich had played at Worcester Academy, the same Massachusetts prep school that had given Maryland Obinna Ekezie, another developing big man who did wonders for the team's grade-point average. Mardesich had needed time for his skills to catch up to his height, and had considered Harvard coming out of Conroe High in Houston in 1995. Born in Long Beach, California, Mardesich had lived on both coasts.

Calvert Hall cited Juan Dixon as a prominent graduate, but the all-Atlantic Coast Conference guard had begun his high school career in Baltimore City, at Lake Clifton. Terence Morris, the team's other established star, was an anomaly. Rather than attend a Maryland football game at Byrd Stadium on a Saturday afternoon in the fall, he preferred to hang out at the Francis Scott Key Mall in Frederick. A homebody who didn't yet have any tattoos or earrings, Morris had spent four seasons at Thomas Johnson High, where his major influence was Tom Dickman. If not for the

Lonny Baxter, Terence Morris, and Byron Mouton (clockwise from lower left) provided strong interior defense when Maryland ended the 2000–2001 regular season with a 35-point romp over Virginia. That game added to the momentum that the Terps took into the postseason. (Baltimore Sun.)

The hard-driving Steve Blake gave the Terps the direction they needed at the point guard position. By his sophomore season, he was well on his way to becoming Maryland's all-time assists leader. (Baltimore Sun.)

Patriots' coach, who has seven state championships and a strong personality, Morris might have listened to Stu Vetter's sales pitch and gone to nearby St. John's Prospect Hall, which used Damien Wilkins and other imports during its brief run among the nation's top prep schools.

How does a coach unite such different young men and guide a long-suffering program to its first trip to the Final Four? Sometimes solid citizens can band together and rally around a common goal. Sometimes they need adversity that forces them to find strength in each other, and on February 14, 2001, Maryland had to circle its wagons.

With its entire eight-man rotation returning from a Top 20 team and Mouton and Wilcox added to the roster, Maryland was ranked sixth in the preseason, but the Terps came out soft in the Maui Invitational and played the turkey on Thanksgiving week. Outhustled by Illinois and Dayton, Maryland returned to the mainland with two losses, and the skid continued in the ACC–Big Ten Challenge in Milwaukee, against Wisconsin. Sun or snow, Maryland was playing miserably, with little emotion.

Williams, who two years earlier had gone against his track record and benched Ekezie, made another tortured lineup switch. Mouton replaced Danny Miller at small forward, and others seemed to find themselves during an easier stretch of the schedule. Maryland saved face in a loss to North Carolina at Cole on January 10, when it rallied from a 19-point deficit and got within three in the final minute. The Terps swatted aside Florida State, Wake Forest, and N.C. State, the Seminoles and the Wolfpack on the road, but then Williams's nemesis came to Cole.

Just as some of Lefty Driesell's teams had seemed to quake at the sight of North Carolina and Dean Smith, Williams's were used to doing the same against Duke and Mike Krzyzewski. Even in the rare seasons when they weren't contending for the NCAA title, the Blue Devils dominated the Terps. Maryland's win at Cameron Indoor Stadium on February 9, 2000, ended a four-game losing streak in Durham. Before that upset, the Blue Devils had won 29 of the last 34 meetings in the series. Two of the Terps' wins came in 1995, when Krzyzewski was on sick leave.

Many of Maryland's losses to Duke had been embarrassments, but the Terps were buoyed by the previous season's win in Durham and ready when the Blue Devils came to Cole Field House on January 27, 2001. Heating up after a slow start, the Terps raced to a 46-37 halftime lead, maintained the pace, and took a 90-80 lead into the final minute of regulation. It was shaping up as a grand weekend for Williams. For only the second time at Cole, he was going to beat a ranked Duke team. ESPN was sending his triumph across the nation. In the morning he would jet to Tampa, Florida, to take in his first pro football championship game, the Baltimore Ravens' rout of the New York Giants in Super Bowl XXXV.

Life was good, until Blake was whistled for his fifth foul and disqualified with 1:51 remaining. Blake had done a splendid job on Jason Williams, Duke's superb point guard, and Maryland didn't really have a backup at the position. Dixon had played some there the previous season, but when Blake needed a break, sophomore Drew Nicholas moved to the point. He was not yet comfortable there, and now Duke and Williams were coming and he couldn't stop them, as the Terps collapsed and the crowd cringed. Williams scored eight points in 13 seconds, as Nicholas failed at the free-throw line and against a double team. Nate James, one of those St. John's Prospect Hall products, got the free throws that forced overtime, and Maryland seemed fortunate to have a shot at a second overtime. Dixon briefly got open before Shane Battier blocked his attempt with the kind of effort that made him the National Player of the Year.

Gary Williams had some explaining to do after a loss that was the most devastating of any he had suffered in three decades of regular-season play. Four days later at Virginia, the Terps spent long stretches in a lifeless trance, and they lost by 21 points. Maryland righted itself against a hapless Clemson club, but road games at Georgia Tech and North Carolina went poorly, and the Terps looked forward to an easy game at Cole against Florida State, another of the ACC's soft touches.

With Baxter revisiting his foul troubles, Morris lost at the offensive end, and Florida State playing with more energy, the Seminoles held on for a 74-71 victory. It would go down as Maryland's final loss at Cole, and it was one of the biggest road wins of Steve Robinson's five seasons in

Tallahassee. Guard Delvon Arrington hopped onto the scorer's table to celebrate. It was futile to put a positive spin on the loss. The game was not sold out, fans fumed, and Williams was defensive when he spiced the postmortem on the radio broadcast with sarcastic thanks for all the support for a program that had gone to seven straight NCAA tournaments.

An eighth straight appearance was in jeopardy. Maryland had a 14-9 record and losses in five of its past six games, and if the Florida State game had come on a weekend instead of a Wednesday, the Terps would have been bounced from the Top 25 for the first time since 1997–98. The NCAA men's basketball committee gives extra weight to a team's finish when it selects and seeds the 65-team tournament, and if Maryland didn't turn around quickly, it would weigh an NIT bid come March 11, Selection Sunday. Williams's critics had a grand time on radio talk shows and Internet chat rooms. With the Terps in the midst of their worst slump in four seasons, wasn't it obvious that Maryland had gone as far as it could under him?

Debates also raged over once mundane matters. Wilcox had gotten the only start of his freshman season against Florida State and played quite well. He was raw, alternating breathtaking finishes with dunks that

Terence Morris did a little of everything for Maryland in a stellar four-year career. The senior got his game going in the NCAA tournament with a strong finish on Georgia State. (Baltimore Sun.)

caromed off the rim to midcourt, but fans loved his energy. The Miller-Mouton question at small forward resurfaced. Dixon had made just three of his 11 shots against the Seminoles, but fans thought worse of Baxter and Morris, the ACC Preseason Player of the Year, who had made just two of his six shots against Florida State. Maryland was a team in crisis, and Williams weighed the possibility that one of his most talented teams ever might not win another game against a demanding schedule down the stretch.

Faced with two of the worst days of his tenure, Williams eased up on his players and told them to forget about the pressure of making the NCAA tournament and have some fun at Wake Forest. With only their most loyal backers in tow at Winston-Salem, Baxter took over the game in the second half and Maryland put on a clinic. Back at Cole, Dixon dropped 30 points on N.C. State, then 23 on Oklahoma after shedding some tight Nikes at halftime.

The Terps had some bounce back in their step when they headed to Duke on February 27. Depending upon affiliation, the January 27 meeting had been a collapse or a comeback, and ESPN scheduled several replays of the "Instant Classic." The rematch was to be the final home game for Battier and James, and the "Cameron Crazies" prepared to send them out in style against their old foils. Duke led 50-43 at the half and 60-51 with 15:20 left, but then strange things began to happen.

Duke center Carlos Boozer left with a broken foot. Most visitors cower in Cameron, where the students seem inches from the court, but Dixon was expert at creating openings in tight spaces and relished the atmosphere there. His floater in the lane with six minutes remaining put Maryland ahead for good. Miller, the returning starter who had been relegated to a reserve role, got the back of his hand on a missed free throw by Baxter for a play-of-the-day put-back. Krzyzewski tried to extend Battier's last home game and forge another comeback, but Maryland made 10 of its last 11 free throws and won by 11.

Its bandwagon back and packing Cole for the regular season finale, Maryland toyed with No. 7 Virginia and matched its most lopsided win ever over the Cavaliers, 102-67. Its momentum reached six straight wins with an 18-point pounding of Wake Forest in the first round of the ACC tournament, which set up round three with Duke at the Georgia Dome in Atlanta. With over 40,000 in attendance, Maryland shot 48.5 percent from the field, but Duke stayed in it with 12 three-pointers. The Terps took an early lead, but needed Blake's three-pointer with 8.1 seconds left to tie. Jason Williams rushed up the court and missed a runner in the lane, but James was there to tip in the rebound for an 84-82 edge with 1.3 ticks left. Dixon somehow got off a decent three-point attempt as the buzzer sounded, but it bounced out.

Duke had the victory, and more regard for Maryland than ever. The combatants collapsed into each other's arms after a game that had the feel of a heavyweight fight. At the end of *Rocky,* Apollo Creed told Rocky Balboa that there wasn't going to be a rematch. In Atlanta, players hugged and said see you in Minneapolis, at the Final Four.

On Selection Sunday, the good news was that the Terps were a No. 3 seed, considered one of the 12 best teams in the nation by the NCAA. The bad news was that Maryland was dispatched to the West Regional for the fourth time in seven seasons, and that there were familiar dangers waiting in Idaho.

Three of the eight teams slated to play in Boise were from the Washington, D.C., metropolitan area and Hampton University was located less than a three-hour drive to the south. Maryland's first-round foe was George Mason, which had a No. 14 seeding and an Army veteran named George Evans who had served in the Gulf War. He outplayed Baxter, but George Mason missed a three-pointer at the end of regulation that would have forced overtime and Maryland escaped with an 83-80 win.

Maryland exhaled, until it considered its second-round opponent. Georgia State was an 11th-seeded upstart from Atlanta with little basketball tradition, but the Terps knew of the Panthers. In the first round they had knocked off Wisconsin, which had beaten Maryland back in November. Georgia State's athletic director was Greg Manning, a Terps player from 1977–81 and their radio analyst for 13 seasons. Then there was the coach: Lefty Driesell, who had picked up a never-was program in 1997 with an assortment of junior college transfers and hand-me-downs who couldn't cut it in major conferences. Maryland was more equipped to confront its past than Driesell, and Baxter made the most of his second chance as the Terps romped by 19.

The road to the Final Four remained familiar at the Pond in Anaheim, California, where Maryland's third-round foe was Georgetown. John Thompson, who had scheduled the Terps once since they met in the NCAA tournament in 1980, was no longer coaching the Hoyas, but Craig Esherick had a big, strong lineup that recalled some of Georgetown's best teams. In the backcourt, Baltimore native Kevin Braswell was close to Dixon, but his friend had better support, as balance and a zone defense got Maryland a 76-66 victory and its first regional final since 1975.

Williams had never coached a game this deep into the NCAA tournament, but Baxter's focus grew sharper the closer the Terps got to the

Tahj Holden's three-point shooting made a difference in the West Region final against Stanford, when the Terps earned their first Final Four berth, but the versatile sophomore could also muscle his way inside. (Baltimore Sun.)

Final Four. Top-seeded Stanford had a hot-shot wing named Casey Jacobsen and two 7-footers in the Collins twins, Jason and Jarron, but Baxter schooled them inside and Miller came off the bench to cool Jacobsen. Tahj Holden gave Maryland a ten-point lead at the half with a three-pointer in front of the Stanford bench, and Baxter finished off the Cardinal with a move they didn't expect, as he split a double team and went up and under with his left hand. Maryland's 87-73 victory represented its high-water mark in 18 appearances in the NCAA tournament.

"You can say you're good enough to get to the Final Four, but until you do, there's a tremendous ceiling you have to really work hard to break through," Williams said later that year. "Nobody here believed we could do it. There weren't a lot of people here with great dreams. We had to create dreams. I'm sure a lot of people thought, 'He's all talk' when I said we could be as good as anybody and compete for a national championship. Getting to the Final Four substantiated that."

On to the Hubert H. Humphrey Metrodome, in Minneapolis, where winter still had a hold on the North Country. It wasn't New Orleans or one of the other tourist destinations that are included in the Final Four rotation, but it was Maryland's first trip to college basketball's biggest weekend, and the Terps' temperature rose at the mention of their semifinal opponent.

It was Duke, the program that had caused Maryland so much misery, the Duke that was the darling of the national media. The more the tournament's bracket filled in, the eerier the Terps' task had become. Driesell had been in the way in the second round and Georgetown in the third, and now the Blue Devils awaited them.

Some Maryland fans had gotten ugly after the loss to Duke at Cole, and athletic director Debbie Yow and others had made a plea for kinder, gentler behavior. The pep band would no longer play "Rock and Roll Part II," a nonsensical Top 40 song from the 1970s to which Terp fans added, "You suck" and "We're gonna beat the hell out of you." As Arizona completed a rout of defending champion Michigan State in the first NCAA semifinal on March 31, its band broke into the song. Maryland fans high-fived and shouted their traditional lines, to the puzzlement of anyone who had never set foot in Cole.

Maryland dominated Duke, but only for 13 minutes. A three-point shot by Blake gave the Terps a 39-17 lead, but if any team in the nation could come back it was the Blue Devils, and besides, the team that led at the half that season in what had become one of college basketball's best rivalries always lost. Duke scored 22 points in the next six minutes. A three-pointer by Dixon extended the Terps' halftime lead to 49-38, but in less than two minutes Morris had picked up his second and third fouls. The first of the two sent Jason Williams to the line, and it was the kind of call that fueled the conspiracy theorists who said that referees favored Duke. When Morris got his fourth foul 14 seconds into the second half, however, there was no one to blame. Caught on a switch on the left side, Morris was beaten to the glass by Battier and clearly went over his back.

Dixon's fourth three-pointer gave him 19 points and the Terps a seven-point lead with 10:40 left, but he was blanked the rest of the way. Boozer, whose low-post skills had led Gary Williams to make a recruiting trip to Alaska, returned from his foot injury to bang inside with Baxter. The two bumped each other all night, and Baxter couldn't believe it when he was called for leaning on Boozer as the two jockeyed for position on a Duke possession. Boozer's two free throws put Duke ahead to stay with 4:43 left. Out of gas, Maryland went more than three crucial minutes without a basket and lost, 95-84.

It was another historic Saturday for Maryland and Williams. In Anaheim, the Terps had put his alma mater into its first Final Four. In Minneapolis, Maryland's 22-point lead turned into the biggest collapse ever at the Final Four.

20

FOR THE SECOND STRAIGHT YEAR, Maryland limped out of Minneapolis an emotional wreck, as Gary Williams, his staff, and his players searched for solutions.

A few hours after their devastating loss to Duke, the Terps fled Minnesota, very early on April Fools' Day, 2001. It was not a restful flight for Kurtis Shultz, the strength and conditioning coach. He had been hired in 1999, after St. John's had pushed around Maryland in the NCAA tournament. Other than making a big steal in the 1993 win over Georgetown, the DeMatha grad had been a nondescript reserve during his time with the Terps, and he was better known as a personal trainer. Shultz's clientele included Ray Lewis and Shannon Sharpe, the most famous members of the world-champion Baltimore Ravens, but he had plenty of projects to keep him busy in College Park.

Shultz was trying to sleep when a long, lean 18-year-old shook his shoulder. It was Chris Wilcox. The freshman forward wanted to know what he had to do to get stronger, and how soon he could start. Wilcox had played just six minutes in the Final Four, and saw that for all of the raves about Shane Battier's leadership skills and three-point shooting, the Duke senior also had a rippled physique.

Wilcox returned to his seat. Shultz tried to close his eyes, but another player stopped at his row. It was Juan Dixon, who repeated Wilcox's concerns.

A year later to the day, Dixon's will, Wilcox's bursting potential, and the talent and intangibles supplied by ten of their teammates gave Maryland basketball its finest hour. As the Terps moved from Cole Field House to the new Comcast Center, they got an arena that had all the amenities that $127 million could buy, plus a neat hanging that had been paid for with blood, sweat, and tears: a national championship banner.

The Terps knew they had the talent to win an NCAA title, but they had to develop new chemistry. Terence Morris took all of his skills to the Houston Rockets, where his teammates included Steve Francis and Walt Williams. Mike Mardesich graduated, and that senior class also took the charisma of LaRon Cephas. In 1999, after Danny Miller's freshman season, there had been rumors that he might transfer to Delaware, where Mike Brey had coached his brother. Now Miller had one college season left, and he didn't want to spend it behind Mouton. He transferred to Notre Dame, where Brey was now coaching. Since McDonald's had added an All-America team to its menu in 1978, no college had won an NCAA title without having at least one of the 30 high schoolers its panel of experts considered the nation's best. Miller had been Maryland's only McDonald's All-American.

There had been a method to the madness of Williams's recruiting philosophy: Top players select established powers, so go after the ones who aren't finished products and develop them. Top 10 teams hadn't exactly banged down the doors to get Dixon and Lonny Baxter, but Williams liked players who had to work to make something of themselves. He had maintained a distant relationship with the D.C. Assault, the region's top AAU team, and the bigger a recruit's entourage, it seemed, the less interest he got from Maryland.

The Terps suffered one other personnel loss. Billy Hahn, Williams's longtime lieutenant, used the 2001 Final Four as a springboard to La Salle, which hired him to make the Explorers a factor in Philadelphia's Big Five again. Williams kept the job in the family, as Matt Kovarik was added to the staff.

All associated with the Terps were obsessed with giving Cole a grand finale and winning the NCAA title. Baxter was motivated every day by the Duke loss in Minneapolis. Its memory meant that a hot date for Dixon and his girlfriend was a night out at a lighted court. Winter meant midnight at Cole, honing his already dangerous stroke with several hundred jumpers, a ritual that Nicholas and others joined.

Basketball became an afterthought on September 11, when terrorists hijacked four jets and the Washington, D.C., area became a war zone. Two of the jets crashed into the World Trade Center in New York, a third was piloted into the Pentagon, and fatalities numbered in the thousands. Less than two weeks later, a tornado touched down near Byrd Stadium, killed two female students, and caused considerable damage. Three days later, Steve Francis helped out by feeding over 100 misplaced students, including 5 basketball players.

Three weeks later, Midnight Madness was staged one last time at Cole. A No. 2 preseason ranking and the Terps' earliest opener ever stoked expectations, which were immediately diminished by a loss to Arizona in the Coaches vs. Cancer Classic at Madison Square Garden. The Wildcats were the Final Four team that was supposed to need rebuilding, but it was the Terps who looked tentative. Suddenly the football team was the toast of the campus. With Ralph Friedgen finally back in the fold as head coach, the Terps went 10-1 during the regular season and clinched their first ACC title since 1985.

Maryland made amends with an impressive win over No. 2 Illinois, the highest-ranked team ever to challenge the Terps' nonconference winning streak at Cole. They looked solid against a younger but gifted Connecticut team in the championship game of the BB&T Classic, but the celebration was short-lived. After the game, Mouton was notified that the previous night in Houston, his older brother Kevin had been shot and killed. Mouton spent five days with his family back in Rayne, Louisiana, and the most demonstrative member of the team leaned on Dixon, who knew too well the loss of loved ones.

On December 21 the unsettled Terps suffered a 16-point loss at Oklahoma, which itself had the makings of a Final Four team. The Sooners' front line was quicker and more aggressive than the Terps, and that setback hastened a change in Williams's rotation. Wilcox lacked inside knowledge but had the most professional potential on the team, and he remained a reserve for only one more game. Williams decided that his talent outweighed his inexperience, and put him in the starting lineup on December 30, for the ACC opener at N.C. State.

Wilcox started every game the rest of the way, and his ability to block shots, run, dunk, and toss in a baby hook was magnified in big games and marveled at by the fans. "The thing I like to do most is get the crowd into the game," he told Josh Barr of the Washington Post. "When you dunk, they say it's only two points, but it turns into six points because it gets everybody hyped. I think that helps us out a lot, to have some action and to have some fun."

Maryland's five-game winning streak ended at Duke, but the Terps quickly got on another roll. January concluded with a steely-eyed 91-87 win at Virginia. With Maryland down nine and 3:22 left, junior guard Drew Nicholas came off the bench and hit two long three-pointers. Silencing hecklers who had chanted "crack-head parents," as he recounted to ESPN magazine, Dixon scored the go-ahead basket with 31 seconds remaining. Ranked No. 4 in the nation at one point, Virginia never recovered from that loss and did not make the NCAA tournament.

Maryland had a seven-game winning streak, but its resumé included three straight losses to Duke when the Blue Devils came to Cole on February 17 with the No. 1 ranking and a 23-1 record. Francis was in the house for a pregame ceremony that added his number to the honor roll of All-Americans whose jerseys were already hanging from the rafters. Seemingly in his honor, the Terps played at a delirious pace, and Wilcox's

13th start was his real coming-out party. When Dixon didn't spend his nights shooting, he scouted game tapes, and he had lobbied Williams to check Duke's Mike Dunleavy with Wilcox instead of the smaller Mouton. Beginning a pattern that would repeat itself at the Final Four, Wilcox scored 23 points and shut down a player with a bigger reputation.

Ninety minutes before the game, the Maryland student section had serenaded Dunleavy's father with an obscene chant, and the crowd figured in the outcome, too. As the first half wound down, Jason Williams couldn't hear the instructions of coach Mike Krzyzewski and looked back to his bench a second time. Steve Blake swooped in, stole the ball from the National Player of the Year, and scored at the buzzer for a 38-29 lead. It grew to 25 points but then shrank to 13, as throats got dry and Cole grew quiet. Dixon alleviated the anxiety with a short jumper, and Maryland won, 87-73.

In the locker room was a floral arrangement sent by a Duke backer, which had been intended to express mock condolences over what would surely be another Blue Devil win. After the Terps' most lopsided win over Duke in 20 years, Williams entered and informed his players that his father, William, 85, had died the day before. The father of assistant coach Dave Dickerson had died the day before the season opener; Mouton was still coming to grips with the murder of his brother, and all that grief made the Terps lean on each other a little more.

"A team takes on a certain part of your life," Dickerson told Gary Lambrecht of the *Sun*. "It pulls you up when you're down, especially when you're close. It's a different bond than the one I have with my wife. Being a part of a team sometimes takes away the exterior stuff. Being around a team sometimes takes everything else away."

The toppling of Duke was the Terps' sixth defeat of a top-ranked team at Cole, which had two emotional games left.

On February 24, the oversized jerseys of Baxter and Dixon were unrolled from the rafters before Maryland played Wake Forest. A misty-eyed Williams rushed to the locker room, lest anyone see him crying over one of the most productive tandems in the program's history. Wake Forest played gallantly, but the Demon Deacons took a time out when they had none, and Dixon's technical free throw made the difference in a 90-89 win.

Now there was just one more game to go at Cole, one last chance for Maryland fans to cram through the narrow concourse and take in their Terps in one of college basketball's shrines. Virginia was the victim March 3, as a 112-92 victory put a neat bow on an unparalleled regular season and 47 seasons at Cole. It gave the Terps a 15-1 record in the ACC, their best ever. It left them 25-3, their best regular-season record ever. It made Maryland 15-0 at Cole, its fourth perfect season there. It ran the Terps' all-time record at Cole to 486-151, and anyone who tried to beat the traffic was a fool.

The send-off started at halftime, when Bud Millikan and two of his teams, the crew that had opened the field house in 1955 and the group that had gone to the NCAAs in 1958, were honored. Men in their sixties squeezed into commemorative jerseys. Some returned after the game, when the Cole floor turned into a Court of Dreams.

There was disappointment that Lefty Driesell hadn't been invited, but dozens of Terps participated in a ceremony in which the ball was passed from basket to basket. Bob Kessler, the big man who had averaged 20.4 points the season Cole opened and had gone on to become an airline pilot, drew applause. So did Bob O'Brien, the Terps' second-leading scorer in 1955–56, and Nick Davis, John Nacincik, Charlie McNeil, and Al Bunge, all members of the 1958 NCAA tournament team. There were fine players from the 1960s who had never tasted postseason glory, like Jerry Greenspan, who later played for Philadelphia in the NBA, and Jay McMillen, who has been practicing medicine for nearly three decades in Missouri. The eras changed when Will Hetzel handed the ball to Jim O'Brien, who had made the most famous shot at Cole, the one that beat South Carolina in 1971. He passed to Tom McMillen, a former U.S. congressman, and on it went, from Len Elmore to Mo Howard to Steve Sheppard to Larry Gibson. Another high-scoring era was appreciated as Albert King passed the ball to Ernie Graham, who handed it to Buck Williams. Adrian Branch got it, and feigned a shot, and the noise peaked for Keith Booth.

Baxter shuffled the ball to Dixon, and then Millikan gave it to one of his favorite players, Williams. On it went to Tahj Holden and Blake, who was picked up by his junior classmate for an impromptu dunk. The former players waved, made their way to the tunnel, and sent the 2001–2 Terps off with a message: Finish it right and win the damned NCAA title!

N.C. State ended Maryland's 13-game winning streak in the semi-finals of the ACC tournament in Charlotte, but lengthy streaks and No. 1 rankings can be a burden in March. The Terps still got their first No. 1 seed, in the East Regional. They disposed of Siena, and followed with a fine effort that wiped out a Wisconsin team that had shared the Big Ten title. If the competition at the MCI Center was not that daunting, an entirely different set of challenges awaited Maryland at the Carrier Dome.

There were no Cinderellas waiting in Syracuse, New York. The Terps' third-round foe was fourth-seeded Kentucky, with seven NCAA titles to its credit. Mouton's defense slowed Tayshaun Prince, and a three-pointer by Nicholas put Maryland ahead for good. Next up was Connecticut, the Big East Conference tournament champion. Even if the Terps hadn't beaten the Huskies three months earlier, the game would have had a familiar feel. Williams and Connecticut coach Jim Calhoun had gone against each other in Boston in the 1980s. Calhoun's first empire, at Northeastern University, had been built on talent from Baltimore's Cecil-Kirk Recreation Center, like the late Reggie Lewis. Now another kid who had played at Cecil-Kirk was about to end his season.

Dixon didn't shoot much in the warm-ups. He methodically bounced the ball, caressed it, and gazed into the stands, then repeated the ritual as he seemed to assess the weight of the game. He was about to put his mark on the tournament.

With sophomore forward Caron Butler playing brilliantly, Williams constantly changing defenses, and Calhoun countering his every move, the Huskies took a 77-74 lead into the final four minutes. A dream season was in serious jeopardy as the Terps worked the ball around the perimeter, looking for a good shot. Dixon collected it at the top of the key. Marked closely by Taliek Brown, Dixon never put the ball on the floor. He rocked Brown off balance with a shoulder fake, and squared his shoulders for a three-pointer from NBA range. With just four seconds left on the 35-second clock, Dixon drained what might have been the biggest pressure shot in Maryland history.

Connecticut wasn't done, and Williams plotted strategy with 35 seconds left and a three-point lead. As he drew up a play to free Dixon or Baxter, Blake interrupted and pointed out that the seniors would be covered, and he would be open for the shot. Held without a basket for more than 39 minutes, the junior point guard delivered a clinching three-pointer. "It put a dagger in them," Blake said. Dixon had admired Blake since the two had tested each other with elbows during a pick-up game in September 1999, and he shook his head and called his backcourt partner "crazy." A lesser team would have folded, but veterans enabled Maryland to score on its last eight possessions in what might have been the best game of the college basketball season. Mouton was a month shy of his 24th birthday. Baxter and Dixon were 23. Blake was 22. Wilcox was still a teenager, but he was playing like a man. They were a seasoned bunch, and engaging, too, with personalities from big cities and the bayou. The starters were not the most quotable—Baxter was cut from the mold of Robert Parish, the former Boston Celtics center who had been dubbed "Chief" for his wooden-Indian ways—but the bench delivered sound bites along with minutes. Holden, who handled his demotion from the starting lineup well, had the self-deprecating wit he'd had since high school, when he had acknowledged that he was "no Corey Maggette." Nicholas's Long Island accent seemed more suited to the lacrosse team. Ryan Randle, the junior forward from Texas and Allegany Community College, joked about the Terps' being "Burger King All-Americans." Williams cracked that walk-on Earl Badu, who planned to attend law school, would earn more as an agent than as a player.

Fittingly, Maryland's historic season concluded in Atlanta, where there were numerous links to the Terps' past. When Millikan had left College Park in 1967, he had opened a branch office for a Baltimore developer in nearby Stone Mountain. Driesell was the coach at Georgia State, about a mile from the Georgia Dome.

Driesell's downfall at Maryland had revolved around a singular talent, the late Len Bias, but this Terp team had a distinctive player, too. Dixon was the only player in NCAA history to reach 2,000 points, 300 steals, and 200 three-pointers. His flair for the dramatic seemed to increase as the tournament progressed. Dixon had begun with 29 points against Siena. He had scored another 29 and broken Bias's career scoring record against Wisconsin. He had earned 19 points against Kentucky, the 1998 champion, and 27 against Connecticut, the 1999 champion, and might have beaten out Baxter for East MVP if ballots hadn't been collected with five minutes remaining.

Now the opponent was the only other top seed to get to the Final Four, two-time champion Kansas. The Jayhawks were the top-scoring team in the nation, but Wilcox intimidated first-team All-American Drew Gooden and Dixon just kept running to shooting daylight. Coach Roy Williams switched defenders in a futile search for someone who could slow Dixon, who matched his career high with 33 points and settled his teammates when the Jayhawks rallied from 20 down to get within four in the closing minutes.

Maryland's 97-88 win over Kansas meant that the Terps were the first team to meet the highest possible seed in each of their first five games and reach an NCAA final. They weren't a surprise, but Indiana was. The Hoosiers had gotten past fellow upstarts North Carolina–Wilmington and Kent State, but they had also beaten trendy favorite Oklahoma in the first game at the Final Four. Most important to Maryland fans, Indiana had eliminated defending champion Duke in the South semifinals. As good as the Terps had felt about blowing out the Blue Devils at Cole, as long as Duke loomed in the other half of the bracket, Maryland was reminded of its meltdown at the 2001 Final Four. The aftermath of the Duke upset had been uneasy for Dickerson, as Hoosier coach Mike Davis thanked him for a scouting report, not that taking the ball to the basket against the Blue Devils was insider trading. Coaches swap information all the time; they just don't discuss it at press conferences.

The Terps seemed exhausted on Easter, the day between the semifinals and the title game. As they were being shuttled by golf cart from a press conference to yet more interviews, Blake rested his head on Baxter's shoulder and yawned. For the 100th time, Dixon told his life story to strangers. Thirty-three hours later, he gave it the happiest possible ending.

Indiana, a five-time champion, had never lost an NCAA final. Maryland had never been this far before, but the Terps liked another pattern, as the program's 2002nd game would be played in the 2002 final. The Maryland pep band's playing of the national anthem was made more stirring by the Port Authority Police Department of New York, which presented the colors, a flag that had flown over the World Trade Center on September 11.

CBS paid Maryland a compliment by putting its lead announcing team of Jim Nantz and Billy Packer on each of its NCAA games, but the latter didn't win any Terp fans by dissecting as sloppy an NCAA championship game that anyone could recall. Defensive work had much to do with the ragged style, and Williams had never cared about style points anyway. His Terps had beaten Kansas at the Jayhawks' game, transition. They would have to beat Indiana at its pace, and Maryland, once a one-trick, run-and-press pony, was finally equipped for a half-court battle.

Dixon personally outscored Indiana in the first nine minutes as the Terps took a 19-8 lead, but then Hoosier defensive stopper Dane Fife kept the ball out of his hands and a football-sized crowd of 53,406 got behind the underdog. Tom Coverdale hit some difficult three-pointers and Indiana took its first lead at 44-42 on a low-post move by Jared Jeffries, but the Terp deficit would last all of seven seconds. Fife gambled and helped out on a trap of Blake, whose NCAA highlights had been restricted to the three against Connecticut. The junior split the double team, took the ball right to the basket, and kicked a laser back to Dixon on the left wing. A few minutes earlier, Dixon had pointed to his brother Phil in the stands and said, "It's all right, it's all right," and he made it right with his first points in 20 minutes, sinking a three-pointer that put Maryland back on top to stay. Jeffries sagged his shoulders as he gathered the ball. Two possessions later, Dixon beat Fife with an outrageous fadeaway jumper, which began a decisive 17-3 spurt. Baxter and the inside game took over, Mouton got to every loose ball, and Indiana seemed to remember that it was a team with 11 losses.

Williams tried to stay in the moment as the clock wound down, but hundreds of games and dozens of people crowded into his thoughts. There were all the gyms he had worked in, the group that had endured NCAA sanctions, and Baxter and Dixon, "what they were and what they are now." Wilcox mussed Williams's hair, and it seemed destiny that at the end of a 64-52 victory, Dixon had the ball to heave aloft. Like a good point guard, Blake gathered it for safekeeping. Dixon had averaged 19.3 points in the regular season but 25.8 in the six NCAA games, and his tournament total of 155 points was the highest in 14 years. He hugged Holden, then Baxter, and the two seniors tumbled to the floor.

"I feel like I'm dreaming right now because I'm part of a national championship team," Dixon would say. "A lot of people back home counted me out, didn't give me a chance. It's a great feeling. I'm speechless. I really don't know what to say. I'm going to talk forever."

There was confusion on the floor, too. Williams's grandson David popped his pop-pop with a pompom.

In College Park, the celebration turned into a riot, with bonfires and arrests on Route 1. The next day, one last giddy crowd at Cole greeted the NCAA champions. The four seniors, Baxter, Dixon, Mouton, and Badu, removed a drape from a banner that had been ordered in advance. Earlier that morning in Atlanta, after the best sleepless night of his life, Williams had explained that it would be a few months before the NCAA championship banner decorated the Comcast Center.

"Cole deserves a banner," Williams said. "It's getting one now."

AT THE END OF THE MOST SUCCESSFUL SEASON in the history of Maryland basketball and Cole Field House, the pace slowed for Gary Williams and the Terps, but only by a bit. When the Terps took one last bow at Cole on the afternoon of April 2, 2002, before an appreciative crowd at a national championship pep rally, the unthinkable finally occurred. When he was brought up for a bow, the unflappable Juan Dixon, pound for pound the toughest guy in college basketball, nearly lost his composure and cried.

In the aftermath of Maryland's NCAA championship, members of the national media asked for a do-over, and admitted that the Atlantic Coast Conference had gotten it right: Dixon was the player of the year, not Duke's Jason Williams. Williams changed his name to Jay, and some NBA executives changed their minds about Dixon. "If a guy like that can't play in the league, then there's something wrong with the league," one scout told ESPN. There were few reservations about Chris Wilcox, who confirmed the rumors that he would leave Maryland after two seasons and just 27 college starts. The sophomore insisted that his teammates never teased him about the way his stock escalated as he dominated a succession of All-Americans, but he emerged as the best power forward prospect in the June draft. He had a strange farewell; while family and friends collected his belongings from his dorm room, Wilcox played pick-up with some unwitting teammates.

In other years, the early loss of a talent like Wilcox would have sent Maryland fans into a funk, but most had come to realize it was part of doing business at the pinnacle of college basketball. Besides, the Terps' run to the 2001 Final Four had impressed the high school Class of 2002, and Williams was supposed to bring in his best recruiting class ever. Power forward Travis Garrison was an important catch out of DeMatha, and when 6-9 Jamar Smith followed Steve Francis and Ryan Randle from Allegany Community College to College Park, it had the makings of a class said to be as good as the Len Elmore–Tom McMillen group that came to town in 1970. In 1992, the Terps had been fortunate to get a sniff from the region's top juniors; in 2002 some of the best in the nation listed Maryland among the colleges they were considering. Maryland seemed ready to reside with Arizona and Duke on the plateau where programs reload instead of rebuild.

Williams and his players were feted around the nation, and on May 3 the M Club's Hall of Fame induction ceremony included Albert King and his coach, Lefty Driesell. Most agreed that the homecoming was long overdue for the man who had put Cole on the map of treacherous places to visit. Two weeks later, Williams and his Terps were honored one more time. In a difficult year for his government and the nation, President George Bush told the Terps what their accomplishments had meant to the people on his staff. He was presented with a Maryland jersey that included his name and the number 1, which had actually been worn by Byron Mouton. The president was flanked by two other seniors, Lonny Baxter and Dixon. One had come out of nearby Anacostia High as a big question mark. The other had left Baltimore's Calvert Hall as a skinny one.

Now Baxter and Dixon were dressed in sharp suits, all grown up. En route from Cole Field House to the Comcast Center, they had earned the Terps an invitation to the White House, and given Maryland one more remarkable memory.

Attner, Paul. *The Terrapins: Maryland Football*. Huntsville, Alabama: The Strode Publishers, 1975.

Baker, Kent. *Maryland Basketball: Red White and Amen*. Huntsville, Alabama: The Strode Publishers, 1979.

Callcott, George H. *A History of the University of Maryland*. Baltimore: Maryland Historical Society, 1966.

Cole, Lewis. *Never Too Young to Die: The Death of Len Bias*. New York: Pantheon Books, 1989.

Douchant, Mike. *Inside Sports College Basketball*. Detroit: Visible Ink Press, 1998.

Doyel, Gregg. *Coach K: Building the Duke Dynasty*. Lenexa, Kansas: Addax Publishing Group, 1999.

Elfin, David, and John McNamara. *Cole Classics: Maryland Basketball's Leading Men and Moments*. Waldorf, Maryland: 21st Century Online Publishing, 2001.

Feinstein, John. *A Season Inside: One Year in College Basketball*. New York: Villard Books, 1988.

Lucas, John, with Joseph Moriarty. *Winning a Day at a Time*. Center City, Minnesota: Hazelden Educational Materials, 1994.

McMillen, Tom, with Paul Coggins. *Out of Bounds: How the American Sports Establishment Is Being Driven by Greed and Hypocrisy—and What Needs to Be Done about It*. New York: Simon and Schuster, 1992.

Prouty, John C., ed. *The ACC Basketball Statbook*. Huntingtown, Maryland: Willow Oak Publishing, 1993.

Smith, C. Fraser. *Lenny, Lefty, and the Chancellor: The Len Bias Tragedy and the Search for Reform in Big-Time College Basketball*. Baltimore: The Bancroft Press, 1992.

Telander, Rick. *Heaven Is a Playground*. New York: St. Martin's Press, 1976.

Wetzel, Dan, and Don Yaeger. *Sole Influence: Basketball, Corporate Greed, and the Corruption of America's Youth*. New York: Warner Books, 2000.

Credits: Photographs by the following photographers appear on the text pages listed: Andre F. Chung (*Baltimore Sun*), 141; Doug Kapustin (*Baltimore Sun*), 144, 149, 156, 157; Kenneth K. Lam (*Baltimore Sun*), 134, 159, 162.

Jacket photographs, and the following color plates, are by the photographers listed:

Plate 1 (Gary Williams), by Gene Sweeney, Jr. (*Baltimore Sun*)

Plate 3 (Byron Mouton celebrating), by Kenneth K. Lam (*Baltimore Sun*)

Plate 4 (devastated Lonny Baxter), by Doug Kapustin (*Baltimore Sun*)

Plate 5 (Juan Dixon versus Jason Williams), by Doug Kapustin (*Baltimore Sun*)

Plate 6 (Chris Wilcox dunking), by Doug Kapustin (*Baltimore Sun*)

Plate 7 and rear jacket (former Terp greats), by Lloyd Fox (*Baltimore Sun*)

Plate 8 (Dixon's defense), by Karl Merton Ferron (*Baltimore Sun*)

Plate 9 (Ryan Randle's defense), by Kenneth K. Lam (*Baltimore Sun*)

Plate 10 (Baxter in traffic), by Kenneth K. Lam (*Baltimore Sun*)

Plate 11 and front jacket (Dixon versus Connecticut), by Kenneth K. Lam (*Baltimore Sun*)

Plate 12 (Final Four fans), by Karl Merton Ferron (*Baltimore Sun*)

Plate 13 (Dixon and Nicholas double-team), by Karl Merton Ferron (*Baltimore Sun*)

Plate 15 (Steve Blake passing), by Lloyd Fox (*Baltimore Sun*)

Plate 16 (Baxter blocks Jared Jeffries), by Karl Merton Ferron (*Baltimore Sun*)

Plate 17 (celebration), by Lloyd Fox (*Baltimore Sun*)